Columbia University

Contributions to Education

Teachers College Series

No. 299

AMS PRESS
NEW YORK

STATE CONTROL OF TEXTBOOKS

WITH SPECIAL REFERENCE TO FLORIDA

BY

CLYDE J. TIDWELL, Ph.D.

Teachers College, Columbia University
Contributions to Education, No. 299

Bureau of Publications
Teachers College, Columbia University
NEW YORK CITY
1928

Library of Congress Cataloging in Publication Data

Tidwell, Clyde Jesse, 1889-
State control of textbooks.

Reprint of the 1928 ed., issued in series: Teachers College, Columbia University. Contributions to education, no. 299.
Originally presented as the author's thesis, Columbia.
Bibliography: p.
1. Educational law and legislation--United States --States. 2. Educational law and legislation--Florida. 3. Text-books--United States--States. 4. Text-books--Florida. I. Title. II. Series: Columbia University. Teachers College. Contributions to education, no. 299.
KF4201.Z95T5 1972 379'.156'09759 77-177710
ISBN 0-404-55299-4

Reprinted by Special Arrangement with Teachers College Press, New York, New York

From the edition of 1928, New York
First AMS edition published in 1972
Manufactured in the United States

AMS PRESS, INC.
NEW YORK, N. Y. 10003

ACKNOWLEDGMENTS

I wish to acknowledge my indebtedness to the officials of the several state departments of education who assisted me in the collection of the data herein presented; to Dr. George D. Strayer, Dr. N. L. Engelhardt, and Dr. E. H. Reisner, of Teachers College, Columbia University, for counsel and guidance; and especially to the members of my dissertation committee, Dr. Carter Alexander, Dr. Paul Mort, and Dr. J. R. McGaughy, for their helpful criticism and encouragement.

C. J. T.

CONTENTS

STATE CONTROL OF TEXTBOOKS

WITH SPECIAL REFERENCE TO FLORIDA

CHAPTER I

TRENDS IN TEXTBOOK LEGISLATION SINCE 1895

INTRODUCTION

Textbooks have always been an important part of the machinery of instruction in American schools. Next to the teacher herself textbooks have had a larger part in determining what has been taught and how it has been taught than any other single influence. Indeed, it is probable that in many cases the textbook has had more influence in shaping the curriculum than the teacher has had. Even to-day lessons are assigned in terms of pages of text, and recitations are conducted as examinations on the content of pages assigned.

The reasons for these conditions in American schools are not hard to find. Our teachers are not generally well trained and they must follow the textbook rather closely in self-defense. Competent supervision is frequently lacking to encourage the teacher to break away from the formal text. Courses of study, where they exist, are not always followed. Reference material is scarce, often unsuitable, and inadequate. For these and many other reasons the textbook commonly used in American schools to-day is anything but a book of texts. In practice it is the course of study.

American publishers have been very sensitive to the textbook needs of the schools, and as a result, American textbooks are very much superior to those published in European countries. American books are well printed, well illustrated, and well bound. For the most part, they are written by our leading educational authorities. They should, and probably do, embody fairly well our best educational theory and practice. Competition among publishers is vigorous, and as a result prices of textbooks are low as compared with prices of other types of publications. Good textbooks are plentiful and cheap.

Other evidences of the importance of textbooks may be found in the laws of the various states. More than half the states have laws requiring the exclusive use of uniform series of textbooks adopted for the entire state, and in six other states the area of uniformity is the county. In some states free textbooks must be provided either by the state or by the local community; in others, local communities are permitted to supply free textbooks, if they wish to do so. In seven states laws designed to control or regulate prices of textbooks are in force, and in two states textbooks are printed by the state.

In view of the importance of textbooks in determining what is being taught in American schools to-day, and in view of the extent of state control of, or participation in, textbook selection, the writer of this dissertation considered the subject worthy of more careful attention than it has yet received. Because of the accessibility of a portion of the necessary data, the study has been made with particular reference to the state of Florida.

THE PURPOSE OF THE STUDY

The purpose of this study is to determine the principles which should govern the relationship between the state and the local community with respect to the selection and provision of textbooks in Florida.

THE PROCEDURE

The procedure for determining these principles was as follows:

1. To ascertain and compare the legal status of textbook selection and provision in the several states.

2. To examine the evidence for and against the more important features of these legal regulations, namely: uniformity laws and free textbook laws; and to derive from this evidence criteria for evaluating textbook legislation with special reference to the state of Florida.

3. From the general principle of state responsibility for education, to derive secondary principles which have special reference to textbook selection and provision.

HISTORICAL BACKGROUND

Textbook laws, generally speaking, are concerned with two major problems. One of these problems has to do with uniformity of textbooks; the other has to do with free textbooks. The uniformity problem arose first out of the efforts of our early teachers to work out graded courses of study. Prior to 1850 [1] children brought to school whatever books they happened to have. Instruction was largely individual, and the schools were ungraded. But with the development of graded courses of study and the grading of pupils, uniform textbooks became a necessity. The first laws on the subject directed the patrons of the schools, or the trustees, to agree on a uniform series of textbooks for use in the schools for a given term of years, and parents were required to supply their children with the books thus adopted. Uniformity of textbooks was wholly local. When families moved from one school district to another they usually found that different textbooks were used in the new district. To avoid the expense of buying new books each time a family moved from one district to another, popular demand for state-wide uniformity grew up in the states where most of the moving of families was going on. Cubberley [2] makes the point that "nowhere in the world do people move about as much as they do in the United States." He cites the report made by the California Curriculum Study Committee to show that "only 29.2 per cent of the pupils who reach the eighth grade had continued in the same school system from the first grade, while 28.6 per cent had changed school systems four times or more." Possibly the situation in California is not typical of the country at large, but there can be little doubt concerning the origin of the popular demand for state-wide uniformity of textbooks.

The question of free textbooks arose even earlier than that of uniformity. Philadelphia was the first city to supply free textbooks in its public schools (1818), and Massachusetts was the first state to make free textbooks mandatory throughout the state (1884). The United States Commissioner of Education reported in 1902, as a result of a study [3] made by the United

[1] Cubberley, E. P. *State School Administration,* Chap. XXI, pp. 555-81. Houghton Mifflin, 1927.

[2] *Op. cit.*

[3] *Report of the United States Commissioner of Education,* 1902, Vol. 2, p. 2390.

TABLE 1

LEGAL PROVISIONS RELATIVE TO UNIFORMITY OF TEXTBOOKS AND FREE TEXTBOOKS IN EFFECT IN THE 48 STATES AT FOUR DIFFERENT PERIODS

STATE	1895–1907			1905–1907			1915–1917			1925–1927		
	Area of Uniformity of Textbooks	Free Textbooks		Area of Uniformity of Textbooks	Free Textbooks		Area of Uniformity of Textbooks	Free Textbooks		Area of Uniformity of Textbooks	Free Textbooks	
		Mandatory or Permanent	Source of Funds		Mandatory or Permanent	Source of Funds		Mandatory or Permanent	Source of Funds		Mandatory or Permanent	Source of Funds
Alabama	Local	..	....	State	..	....	State	..	....	State	P	Local[3]
Arizona	State	..	....	State	..	....	State	M	State	State	M	State
Arkansas	Local	..	....	County	..	....	County	..	....	State	P	Local
California	State	..	....	State	..	....	State	M	State	State	M	State[1]
Colorado	Local	P	Local	Local	P	Local	Local	P	Local	District	P	Local
Connecticut	Local	P	Local	Local	P	Local	Local	P	Local	District	P	Local
Delaware	State	M	Local	State	M	Local	State	M	Local	State	M	State
Florida	County	..	....	State	..	....	State	..	....	State	M	State
Georgia	County	..	....	State	..	....	State	..	....	State	P	Local
Idaho	State	P	Local	State	P	Local	State	P	Local	State	P	Local
Illinois	Local	..	....	Local	..	....	Local	..	....	District	P	Local
Indiana	State	..	....	State	..	....	State	..	....	State	..	....
Iowa	County	P	Local	County	P	Local	County	P	Local	County	P	Local
Kansas	State	P	Local	State	P	Local	State	P	Local	State	P	Local
Kentucky	County	..	....	State	..	....	State	..	....	State	..	....
Louisiana	State	..	....	State	..	....	State	..	....	State	..	....
Maine	Local	M	Local	Local	M	Local	Local	M	Local	District	M	Local
Maryland	County	M	County	County	M	County	County	M	County	County	M	State[2]

Massachusetts........	Local	M	Local	Local	M	Local	Local	M	Local	District	M	Local
Michigan............	Local	P	Local	Local	P	Local	Local	P	Local	District	P	Local
Minnesota............	Local	P	Local	Local	P	Local	Local	P	Local	District	P	Local
Mississippi..........	County	..	....	State	..	....	State	..	....	State	P.	Local
Missouri.............	State	..	....	County	P	Local	County	P	Local	County	P	Local[3]
Montana.............	State	..	....	State	P	Local	State	P	Local	State	M	Local
Nebraska.............	Local	M	Local	Local	M	Local	Local	M	Local	District	M	Local
Nevada..............	State	..	....	State	..	....	State	M	Local	State	M	State
New Hampshire........	Local	M	Local	Local	M	Local	Local	M	Local	District	M	Local
New Jersey...........	Local	M	Local	Local	M	Local	Local	M	Local	District	M	Local
New Mexico..........	State	..	....	State	..	....	State	..	....	State	M	State
New York............	Local	P	Local	Local	P	Local	Local	P	Local	District	P	Local
North Carolina........	County	..	....	State	..	....	State	..	....	State	P	Local
North Dakota.........	Local	P	Local	Local	P	Local	Local	P	Local	District	P	Local
Ohio................	Local	..	....	Local	P	Local	Local	P	Local	District	P	Local
Oklahoma............	Local	..	....	Local	..	....	State	..	....	State	P	Local
Oregon..............	State	..	....	State	..	....	State	..	....	State	..	....
Pennsylvania..........	Local	M	Local	Local	M	Local	Local	M	Local	District	M	Local
Rhode Island.........	Local	M	Local	Local	M	Local	Local	M	Local	District	M	Local
South Carolina........	State	..	....	State	..	....	State	..	....	State	..	....
South Dakota.........	County	P	Local	County	P	Local	County	P	Local	County	M	Local
Tennessee............	Local	..	....	State	..	....	State	..	....	State	P	Local
Texas................	State	..	....	State	..	....	State	P	Local	State	M	State
Utah................	State	..	....	State	M	Local	State	M	Local	State	M	Local
Vermont.............	County	P	Local	Local	M	Local	Local	M	Local	District	M	Local
Virginia..............	State	..	....	State	..	....	State	..	....	State	P	Local
Washington...........	State	..	....	State	P	Local	County	P	Local	County	P	Local
West Virginia..........	State	..	....	County	P	Local	State	P	Local	State	P	Local
Wisconsin............	Local	P	Local	Local	P	Local	County	P	Local	County	P	Local
Wyoming.............	Local	..	....	Local	M	Local	Local	M	Local	District	M	Local

[1] Local for high schools. [2] State and County. [3] State Aid.

States Bureau of Education that 93 of the 161 cities then having a population of 25,000 or more were supplying free textbooks to some or all of their pupils.

SUMMARY OF LEGAL PROVISIONS FOR EACH DECADE SINCE 1895-97

This study is concerned not so much with the historical beginnings of uniformity and free textbook laws as it is with the present status of such laws. Nevertheless, in order to discover what the trends are or have been, a study of the textbook laws of each state was made covering a period of thirty years. The essential provisions with reference to uniformity and free textbooks are presented in Table 1 for each state for the years of 1895-97, 1905-07, 1915-17, and 1925-27. Table 2 summarizes Table 1.

TABLE 2

TOTAL NUMBER OF STATES HAVING LEGAL PROVISIONS RELATIVE TO UNIFORMITY OF TEXTBOOKS AND FREE TEXTBOOKS AT FOUR DIFFERENT PERIODS. SUMMARY OF TABLE 1

	1895-97	1905-07	1915-17	1925-27
Area of Uniformity				
State	18	23	24	25
County	9	6	7	6*
Local	21	19	17	17
Free Textbooks				
a. Type of Law				
Mandatory	9	12	15	20
Permissive	12	16	17	23
No laws	27	20	16	5
b. Source of Funds				
State	0	0	2	8
County	1	1	1	0
Local	20	27	29	35

* Optional local or county for one state.

With reference to uniformity, Tables 1 and 2 show that there was a tendency for county uniformity to become state uniformity during this thirty-year period. Only one state (Washington) abandoned state uniformity; it adopted county uniformity. Three states (Alabama, Arkansas, and Tennessee) abandoned local adoptions for state uniformity, and one state

(Vermont) abandoned county uniformity for local adoptions. All of these changes were made by 1917. Since that time there have been no marked changes in the uniformity laws of any of the states, and such changes as have been made do not affect the classification of any state.

During the thirty-year period under consideration there was a decided trend in the direction of mandatory free textbook laws. Twenty states now have such laws, as contrasted with nine in 1895. Twenty-three states have laws which specifically permit the expenditure of public school funds for free textbooks. There is also a definite trend in the direction of free textbooks paid for out of state funds instead of local funds.

In a report made by William R. Hood,[4] Specialist in School Legislation, for the United States Bureau of Education, the facts are given for the states where free textbook laws are permissive and not mandatory. This report is based on replies to questionnaires sent to state departments of education. In some cases the data could not be furnished. It is evident, however, that a considerable proportion of the cities and towns avail themselves of the right to furnish free textbooks, at least in the elementary grades. Free textbooks are not so generally furnished in the high school.

It should be said at this point that practically every state allows or requires free books to be supplied to indigent pupils. It should be said also that many cities have been granted special charters which exempt them from the application of the general provisions of uniformity laws.

EXTENT OF TEXTBOOK UNIFORMITY AND FREE TEXTBOOK LAWS IN EACH STATE

Map 1 shows the geographical distribution of the several states with reference to legal provisions for textbook uniformity. It is apparent that state-wide uniformity prevails very generally in the southern states; that local adoption is the rule in the New England and North Atlantic states; and that "open listing" is the prevailing method of state regulation of textbooks in the northern group of middle-western states. Just what the significance of these rather marked sectional differences may be

[4] *Free Textbooks for Public School Pupils.* U. S. Bureau of Education, Bulletin, 1923, No. 50, pp. 9-10. Washington, D. C., 1924.

is not clear. Various theories might be offered in partial explanation of these facts, but they would be only theories. The explanation of the predominance of state-wide uniformity in the southern states may lie in the fact that these states have not had confidence in the competence of local school leadership. Another possible explanation may be that states tend to imitate their neighbors in respect to legislative enactments.

Map 2 shows the situation with respect to free textbook laws. It will be noted that there is very little, if any, relationship between uniformity laws and free textbook laws so far as individual states are concerned. Free textbooks are mandatory in both uniformity and non-uniformity states, just as they are permissive in both types of states. Nine states which have uniformity laws require free textbooks either for elementary grades or for all grades, while eleven states which have non-uniformity laws make the same requirements with reference to free textbooks.

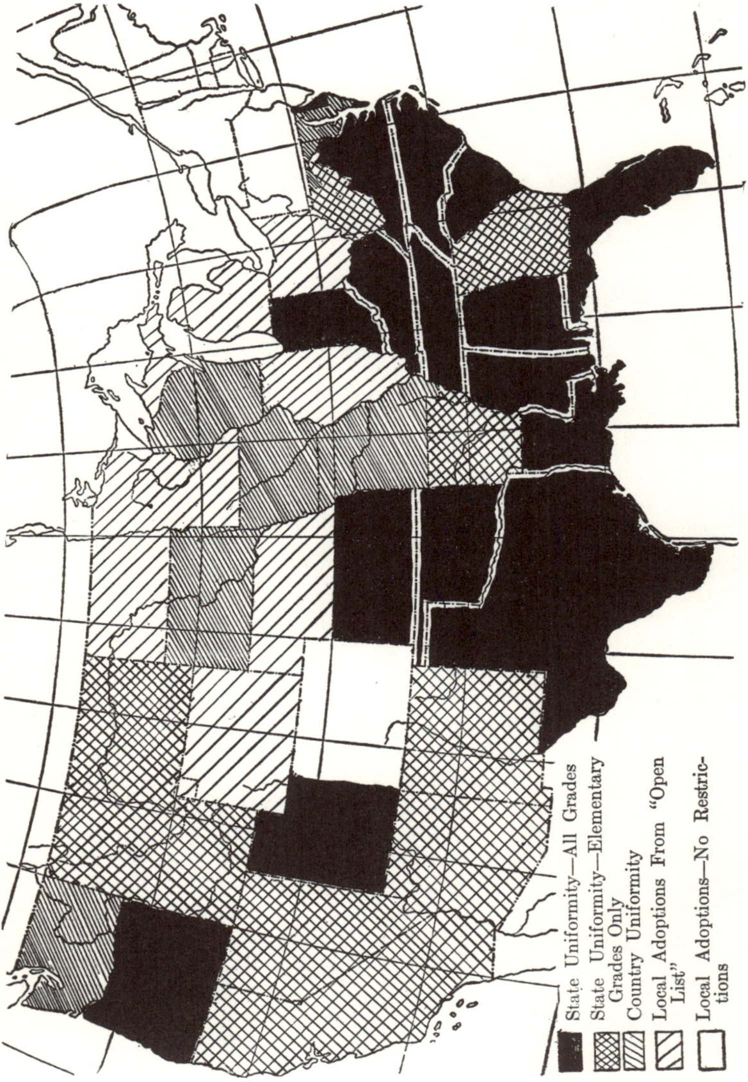

MAP 1

Extent of Textbook Uniformity in Each of the Forty-eight States in 1925-27

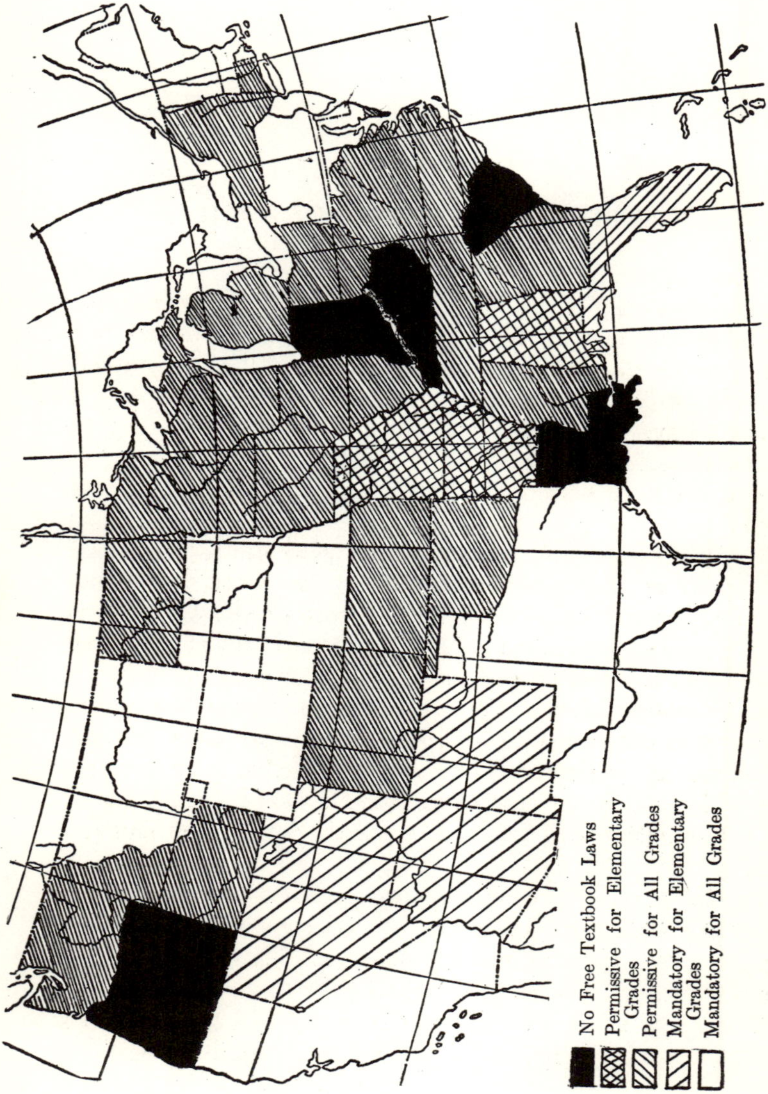

MAP 2

Extent of Free Textbook Laws in Each of the Forty-eight States in 1925–27

CHAPTER II

TEXTBOOK LAWS IN EFFECT IN 1927

In the foregoing chapter it was shown that legislation covering state-wide uniformity of textbooks had apparently reached a state of equilibrium by 1917. Presumably the states are finding the essential provisions of their uniformity laws generally satisfactory. The changes that have been made during the past ten years have had to do with the machinery for making the laws effective, such as changes in methods of determining the adopting body, in administrative procedures, and in legal safeguards.

If, as now seems probable, uniformity laws are to continue in effect so far as their essential provisions are concerned, a comparison of the several state laws may be of some use in shaping future legislation on the subject. Such a study will at least serve to point out adequacies and inadequacies of existing laws. If, out of an examination of the detailed provisions of the several state laws on uniformity, it is possible to discover their desirable and undesirable features, it may then be possible to set up principles which should govern the relations between a state and its local communities with reference to textbook selection and provision.

With this purpose in view, a list of the essential regulations of each of the state laws on textbook selection and provision was compiled. For convenience in tabulating, thirty-three items were selected for classification purposes.

A few minor items were omitted from the list, either because they did not occur frequently enough to warrant inclusion or because they seemed insignificant or irrelevant to the purposes of this study. The list was made up from the latest available state school codes and from state laws which have been passed since the adoption of the latest school codes. Typed copies of the facts thus compiled were sent to all the state departments concerned, with the request that any errors or omissions be

TABLE 3: LEGAL PROVISIONS RELATIVE TO TEXT

	Alabama	Arizona	Arkansas	California	Colorado	Connecticut	Delaware	Florida	Georgia	Idaho	Illinois	Indiana	Iowa	Kansas	Kentucky	Louisiana	Maine	Maryland	Massachusetts	Michigan	Minnesota
A. Adopting Body	(1)			(3)				(1)													
1. *a.* State Board of Education	x	x	..	x	..	..	x	x	x	..	..	x	..	..	..	x	..	..	..	..	..
b. Specially Appointed Board	..	..	x	..	..	..	..	..	..	..	..	..	..	x	x	..	..	..	..	..	..
c. Combination of (*a*) and (*b*)	..	..	..	..	..	..	..	..	..	x	..	..	..	..	..	..	..	..	..	..	..
d. County Board	..	..	..	..	..	..	..	..	..	..	..	..	(9) x	..	..	..	..	x	..	..	..
e. Local Board	..	..	..	..	x	x	..	..	..	..	x	..	..	..		..	x	..	x	x	x
2. Number of Members	7	8	9	10	..	..	4	7	6	5	..	13	..	7	12	11	..	..	..	..	..
3. Term of Office—Years	6	..	6	4	..	..	5	..	4	5	..	4	..	2	4	(11) 8	..	..	..	..	..
4. Compensation per day, $	10	..	5	..	..	..	25	5	..	..	..	5	..	5	..	10	..	..	..	..	..
5. Authority to adopt Uniform Books	x	x	x	(4) x	x	x	x	x	x	x	x	x	x	(10) x	x	x	x	x	(14) x	x	x
6. State Supt. is member of Board	x	x	x	x	..	..	x	x	x	x	..	x	..	x	x	x	..	..	..	..	..
B. Scope and Effect																					
1. Area of Uniformity																					
a. State	x	x	x	x	..	..	x	x	x	x	..	x	..	x	x	x	..	..	..	..	..
b. County	..	..	..	..	..	..	..	..	..	..	..	..	x	..	..	..	..	x	..	..	..
c. District	..	..	..	..	x	x	..	..	..	..	x	..	..	..	..	..	x	..	x	x	x
2. Grades Affected																					
a. Elementary only	..	x	x	x	..	..	..	..	x	x	..	..	..	..	..	..	..	..	..	..	..
b. All	x	..	..	..	x	x	x	x	..	..	x	x	x	x	x	x	x	x	x	x	x
3. *a.* Single List	x	x	x	x	..	..	(6) x	x	x	x	..	(8) x	..	x	x	(12) x	..	(13) x	..	..	..
b. Multiple List	..	..	..	..	..	..	x	..	..	..	..	x	..	..	..	x	..	x	..	..	..
c. Open List	..	..	..	..	..	..	..	..	..	..	x	..	..	..	..	..	..	..	..	x	x
4. Term of Adoption—Years	6	5	6	(4) 8	..	5	4	8	5	6	5	5	..	..	10	6	..	..	..	5	5
5. Special Provisions for																					
a. Periodical revision	..	..	x	x	..	..	..	..	..	..	..	x	..	..	..	..	..	..	..	..	..
b. Dropping unsatisfactory Books	x	..	..	..	..	..	x	..	..	x	..	..	..	..	..	x	..	..	..	..	..
c. Supplementary Books	..	..	x	x	..	x	x	x	..	..	..	..	..	x	x	..	..	x	..	..	..
6. Price Regulations	x	x	x	x	..	..	x	x	x	x	x	x	..	x	x	x	..	x	..	x	x
7. Exchange Regulations	..	..	x	x	..	..	..	x	x	x	x	x	..	x	x	x	..	x	..	..	x
8. Exemptions																					
a. Cities of Specified Class	x	..	..	..	..	..	x	..	x	..	..	..	..	..	..	x	..	x	..	..	..
b. Districts of Specified Class	..	..	..	..	..	..	..	..	x	x	..	..	..	..	..	..	..	..	..	..	..
C. Administrative Safeguards																					
1. Left to Commission	..	..	..	..	..	..	x	..	..	x	..	..	..	x	..	x	..	x	..	..	..
2. Must Advertise for Bids	x	x	x	(29) x	..	..	..	..	x	..	..	x	..	..	x	..	..	..	..	..	..
3. Bond Required	x	x	x	x	..	..	..	x	x	x	x	x	..	..	x	..	..	..	..	x	x
4. Depositories Required	..	x	x	..	..	..	..	x	x	x	..	x	..	x	x	..	..	..	..	..	..
5. Specific Provisions against																					
a. Efforts to influence adoption	x	..	x	..	..	..	..	x	..	..	..	x	..	..	x	..	..	..	..	..	x
b. Combinations to restrain competition	..	x	..	x	..	..	..	..	..	..	x	x	..	..	x	..	..	..	..	..	x
c. Violation of provisions	x	..	x	..	..	..	..	x	x	x	..	x	..	x	x	..	..	..	..	..	..
D. Other General Provisions																					
1. Free Textbooks																					
a. Mandatory	..	x	..	x	..	..	x	x	..	..	..	..	..	..	..	..	x	x	x	..	..
b. Permissive	x	..	x	..	x	x	..	..	x	x	x	..	x	x	..	..	..	..	..	x	x
c. Area Affected																					
(1) State	..	x	..	x	..	..	x	x	..	..	..	..	..	..	..	..	..	..	..	..	..
(2) County	x	..	..	..	..	..	..	..	x	..	..	..	x	..	..	..	..	x	..	..	..
(3) District	x	..	x	..	x	x	..	..	x	x	x	..	x	x	..	..	x	..	x	x	x
d. Source of Funds	(2)			(5)																	
(1) State	x	x	..	x	..	..	x	x	..	..	..	..	..	..	..	..	..	x	..	..	..
(2) County	x	..	..	..	..	..	..	..	x	..	..	..	..	..	..	..	..	x	..	..	..
(3) Local District	x	..	x	x	x	x	..	..	x	x	x	..	x	x	..	..	x	..	x	x	x
e. For what Grades								(7)													
(1) Elementary	x	x	x	x	x	x	x	x	x	x	x	..	x	x	..	..	x	x	x	x	x
(2) High School	..	..	..	x	x	x	x	..	x	x	x	..	x	x	..	..	x	x	x	x	x
f. Provisions for Fumigating	..	x	..	..	..	..	..	x	..	x	..	..	..	..	..	..	..	..	..	..	..
2. Provision for State Printing	..	..	..	x	..	..	..	..	..	..	..	..	..	x	..	..	..	..	..	..	..

1. In Ala. State Textbook Purchasing Board is adopting body. In Fla. the adopting body is the Board of Commissioners of State Institutions. Subcommittees are appointed to recommend list to Commissioners. 2. State aid to furnish free textbooks. 3. For elementary schools. District high school Boards for high school books. 4. Boards may adopt or have printed elementary books; it approves an open list of high school books which are adopted for 8 years. 5. For elementary books only. Local districts pay for high school books. 6. Multiple choice for special districts. 7. Grades 1–6. 8. Multiple choice for certain high school books. 9. Optional; the county is the area of uniformity in the majority of cases. 10. May print or publish as board may decide. 11. For elective members. Four years for appointive members. 12. Optional with State Board. 13. Optional with county supt. 14. Must be approved by local

BOOKS IN EFFECT IN THE 48 STATES, 1925–27

Mississippi	Missouri	Montana	Nebraska	Nevada	New Hampshire	New Jersey	New Mexico	New York	North Carolina	North Dakota	Ohio	Oklahoma	Oregon	Pennsylvania	Rhode Island	South Carolina	South Dakota	Tennessee	Texas	Utah	Vermont	Virginia	Washington	West Virginia	Wisconsin	Wyoming	
..	..	..	..	..	..	..	x	..	(18) x	..	..	..	..	..	..	x	..	..	..	..	..	x	..	x	..	..	13
(15) x	..	x	..	..	..	..	..	..	..	..	..	x	x	..	..	..	..	x	x	x	..	..	..	..	..	..	10
..	..	..	..	x	..	..	..	..	..	..	..	..	..	..	..	..	..	..	..	..	..	..	..	..	..	..	2
..	x	..	..	..	..	..	..	..	..	..	..	..	..	..	..	..	x	..	..	..	..	..	x	..	x	..	6
..	..	..	x	..	x	x	..	x	..	x	x	..	..	x	x	..	..	..	..	..	x	..	..	..	..	x	17
9	3	7	..	7	..	..	7	..	(19) 7	..	..	7	5	..	..	9	5	7	9	9	..	6	5	7	5	..	..
5	2	5	..	4	..	..	4	..	5	..	..	5	4	..	..	4	..	..	..	4	..	4	2	6	5	..	..
(16) 5	5	6	..	5	..	..	5	..	..	..	..	6	..	..	..	10	..	5	5	..	..	..	3	..	..	..	..
x	x	x	x	x	x	x	x	x	x	x	x	x	x	(14) x	x	x	x	x	x	x	(14) x	x	x	x	x	x	48
..	..	..	..	x	..	..	x	..	..	..	..	x	..	..	..	x	..	x	x	..	..	x	..	x	..	..	20
x	..	x	..	x	..	..	x	..	(20) x	..	..	x	x	..	..	x	..	x	x	x	..	x	..	x	..	..	25
..	x	..	..	..	..	..	..	..	..	..	..	..	..	..	..	..	(21) x	..	..	..	..	..	(26) x	..	x	..	6
..	..	..	x	..	x	x	..	x	..	x	x	..	..	x	x	..	..	..	..	..	x	..	..	..	..	x	17
..	..	x	..	x	..	..	x	..	..	..	..	..	..	..	..	..	..	..	..	..	..	..	..	x	x	..	10
x	x	..	x	..	x	x	..	x	x	x	x	x	x	x	x	x	x	x	x	x	x	x	x	..	..	x	38
x	x	x	..	x	..	..	x	..	x	..	..	x	x	..	..	x	x	(22) x	(24) x	(12) x	..	x	x	x	x	..	30
(28) x	..	..	..	..	..	..	..	..	..	..	..	..	..	..	..	..	..	x	x	x	..	..	..	..	..	..	8
..	..	..	x	..	..	..	..	..	..	x	x	..	..	..	..	..	..	..	..	..	..	..	..	..	..	x	7
5	5	6	..	4	..	..	6	5	5	3	5	5	6	5	3	5	5	5	6	6	..	4	(27) 5	5	5	5	..
..	..	..	..	..	..	..	..	..	..	..	x	..	..	..	..	..	..	..	x	..	..	..	..	..	..	..	5
x	..	..	..	..	..	..	..	..	x	..	..	..	..	..	..	..	..	..	..	x	..	..	..	..	..	..	7
..	x	x	..	x	..	..	..	..	..	..	x	x	..	x	..	x	..	x	x	..	..	x	x	x	x	..	21
x	x	x	x	x	..	x	x	..	x	x	x	x	x	..	..	x	x	x	x	x	..	x	x	x	x	x	38
x	x	x	..	x	..	..	x	..	x	x	x	x	..	..	..	x	x	x	x	x	..	x	x	x	x	..	30
(17) x	x	..	..	..	..	..	..	..	..	..	..	..	x	..	..	x	..	..	..	x	..	..	..	x	x	..	12
..	..	..	..	..	..	..	..	..	..	..	..	..	..	..	..	..	x	..	..	..	..	..	x	..	x	..	5
..	..	..	..	..	..	..	x	..	x	..	..	..	..	..	..	x	..	..	..	..	..	x	x	..	..	..	10
x	x	x	..	x	..	..	..	..	..	..	..	x	x	..	..	..	x	x	x	x	..	..	x	x	x	..	20
x	x	x	x	x	..	..	..	..	..	x	..	x	x	..	..	x	x	x	x	x	..	x	..	x	x	x	29
x	..	x	..	x	..	..	..	..	..	..	..	x	x	..	..	x	..	x	x	..	..	x	..	x	x	..	19
..	x	..	..	..	..	..	..	..	..	x	x	x	..	x	..	..	x	x	x	x	..	..	..	x	x	x	18
..	x	..	..	..	..	..	..	..	..	x	..	x	..	..	..	..	..	..	x	..	..	..	..	..	x	x	12
x	x	x	..	x	..	..	..	..	..	x	x	x	x	x	..	x	x	x	x	x	..	x	..	x	x	x	26
..	..	x	x	x	x	x	x	..	..	..	..	..	..	x	x	..	x	..	x	x	(25) x	..	..	..	..	x	20
x	x	..	..	..	..	..	..	x	x	x	x	x	..	..	..	..	..	(23) x	..	..	..	x	x	x	x	..	23
..	..	x	..	x	..	..	x	..	..	..	..	..	..	..	..	..	..	..	x	..	..	..	..	..	..	..	8
x	x	..	..	..	..	..	..	..	x	..	..	..	..	..	..	..	x	..	..	x	..	..	..	..	x	..	10
x	x	..	x	..	x	x	..	x	x	x	x	x	..	x	x	..	..	x	..	x	x	x	x	x	x	x	33
..	(2) x	..	..	x	..	..	x	..	..	..	..	..	..	..	..	..	..	..	x	..	..	..	..	..	..	..	8
x	x	..	..	..	..	..	..	..	x	..	..	..	..	..	..	..	..	..	..	x	..	..	..	..	x	..	8
x	x	x	x	..	x	x	..	x	x	x	x	x	..	x	x	..	x	x	..	x	x	x	x	x	x	x	36
x	x	x	x	x	x	x	x	x	x	x	x	x	..	x	x	..	x	x	x	x	x	x	x	x	x	x	43
x	..	x	x	..	x	x	..	x	x	x	x	x	..	x	x	..	x	x	x	..	x	x	x	x	x	x	35
..	..	..	..	..	..	..	..	..	..	..	..	..	..	..	..	..	..	..	..	..	..	..	..	..	..	..	3
..	..	..	..	..	..	..	..	..	..	..	..	x	..	..	..	..	x	x	..	..	..	..	..	..	..	..	5

supt. 15. Separate commissions for elementary and high schools. 16. $10 for high school commission. 17. On vote of local board may adopt other than state-adopted high school books. 18. Subcommittees for high school and elementary school recommend multiple list to State Board. 19. Five for high school. 20. County for the high schools. 21. For rural schools. Local districts for others. 22. Single for elementary, multiple for high. 23. By special legislation. 24. Multiple for high schools of first class. 25. Permissive for high schools. 26. Local for first division schools. 27. Three years for first division schools. 28. Separate list for different types of high schools. 29. Applies to high school books only.

indicated, and particularly any differences between actual practice and the apparent law. Such corrections or differences as were indicated by the several state departments were incorporated in the summaries of the state laws and it is believed that they are now accurate. To illustrate the form and content of the list of items for which the facts were compiled for each state, a sample summary is reproduced herewith for one state. These summaries are brought together in somewhat abridged form in Table 3, pages 12 and 13.

SUMMARY OF STATE LAWS ON UNIFORMITY OF TEXTBOOKS

Alabama

The Textbook Commission

1. Adopting Body: Textbook Purchasing Board from list recommended by Textbook Committee.
2. Appointed by: State Board of Education on recommendation of State Superintendent.
3. Number of members: 7.
4. Term of office: 6 years.
5. Compensation: $10 per day, plus expense.
6. Personnel: Well-known educators engaged in public school work.
7. Restrictions as to members: May not be interested directly or indirectly in any contract that may be let.
8. Duties and powers: To select three best books in each subject and report to Purchasing Board. Latter Board makes final selection from list.
9. Relation of State Superintendent: Ex-officio chairman.

Scope and Effect

1. Area of uniformity: State.
2. Subjects affected: All.
3. Grades affected: All.
4. Single or multiple choice: Single.
5. Term of adoption: 6 years.
6. Provisions for changing: None.
7. Provisions for revising: None.
8. Provisions for dropping: State Board may drop any book at end of any year if three-fourths of Board vote to do so.
9. Provisions for supplementary books: None.
10. Price Regulations: Maximum sale price to be printed or stamped on each book cover. Covered in contract.
11. Exchange provisions: None.
12. Exemptions: Cities of 40,000 population which furnish free books; and cities of 2,500 population may adopt other high school books with approval of State Board of Education.

Administrative Procedure and Legal Safeguards

1. Commission must advertise for bids: Yes.
2. Sealed bids and deposit required: Yes.
3. Bond required if bid is accepted: Yes, in amount fixed by Purchasing Board.
4. Depositories required: No.
5. Overcharging prohibited: Yes.
6. Efforts to influence adoptions: Prohibited. Secret report of Commission.
7. Combinations in restraint of competition: Not mentioned.
8. Penalties for violation: Yes.
9. Regulations for distributions: By State Board of Administration.

Other General Provisions

1. Free textbooks
   a. Permissive or mandatory: Permissive to districts having 7-month or longer school terms.
   b. For what area: District or county.
   c. Source of funds: District or county. State will contribute 10 per cent of cost of free elementary books.
   d. For what grades: All.
2. Fumigation of books: None.
3. State printing: None.

Table 3 shows that twenty-five states have state-wide uniformity laws; seventeen states have local adoptions; five states have county adoptions; and one state has optional local or county adoptions. Table 4 shows the classification of each of the forty-eight states with respect to general uniformity laws.

A. THE ADOPTING BODY

Referring again to Table 3, it will be seen that the adopting bodies in the states which have state-wide uniformity are of two principal kinds. Eleven of the twenty-five states having state-wide uniformity designate the state board of education as the adopting body; eleven states have specially appointed state textbook commissions; two states employ a combination of the state board and especially appointed members; and in one state (Florida) the board of commissioners of state institutions is the adopting body.

In the states having county uniformity, it is usual for the county board of education to adopt books for the county, while in the non-uniformity states the local board of education is the adopting body.

TABLE 4

CLASSIFICATION OF STATES WITH REFERENCE TO TEXTBOOK UNIFORMITY LAWS

STATE UNIFORMITY	COUNTY UNIFORMITY	LOCAL ADOPTIONS
Alabama	*Iowa	Colorado
Arizona	Maryland	Connecticut
Arkansas	Missouri	Illinois
California	South Dakota	Maine
Delaware	Washington	Massachusetts
Florida	Wisconsin	Michigan
Georgia		Minnesota
Idaho		Nebraska
Indiana		New Hampshire
Kansas		New Jersey
Kentucky		New York
Louisiana		North Dakota
Mississippi		Ohio
Montana		Pennsylvania
Nevada		Rhole Island
New Mexico		Vermont
North Carolina		Wyoming
Oklahoma		
Oregon		
South Carolina		
Tennessee		
Texas		
Utah		
Virginia		
West Virginia		

* Optional local or county uniformity.

Personnel.—The adopting bodies for the uniformity states are generally composed of members engaged in educational work, either by ex-officio designation or by law when the appointment is left to the governor. It is apparent that the law-making bodies of the several uniformity states have had in mind adopting bodies which would be professionally capable and at the same time representative of the various educational interests in the state. In two states (Florida and North Carolina) the law provides definitely for the appointment of special subcommittees which report to the official adopting bodies in those states. In both states separate subcommittees are appointed to select elementary textbooks and high school textbooks. While the recommendations of the subcommittees do not legally bind the adopting bodies, in practice their recommendations are usually followed. In North Carolina the state board of education adopts elementary textbooks from a multiple list recommended by the state textbook commission. It approves books recommended by the state high school textbook commission. It may remove any book from the recommended list, but it may not substitute others.

In Alabama the arrangement is similar to the arrangement in North Carolina. There, the state board of education, on recommendation of the state superintendent, appoints a state textbook committee which recommends three books in each subject to the state purchasing board. The latter board, of which the state superintendent is ex-officio chairman, makes the final selection.

In Idaho, where the legal adopting body is the state board of education and the board of regents of the University of Idaho, the state superintendent reports that in practice the matter of textbook selection is "always delegated to a book committee of teachers and experts for recommendation."

Number of Members.—The number of members composing the adopting bodies varies from three to thirteen, seven being the most common number. Their terms of office range from two years as a minimum to an indefinite maximum, with four years as the most common term. In the case of the subcommittees in North Carolina and Florida the term of office is for one adoption only. The members are discharged after they have made their recommendations.

Compensation.—Compensation allowed the members of the adopting bodies ranges from nothing (probably expenses) to $10 per actual day of service plus expenses. Where the state board of education is ex officio the adopting body the allowance is sometimes higher, but these bodies usually have other duties to perform. In no case is there an allowance which might be used to employ expert advice. It is evident that the members of the several adopting bodies are expected personally to examine the books under consideration and to reach decisions based on such examinations.

Powers and Authorities.—The powers and authorities of the adopting bodies are broad and general. A typical law empowers the adopting body to select, adopt, and enforce a uniform series of textbooks and to contract with the publishers of such books.

In no case does the law attempt to direct the adopting body beyond the general requirement that it consider such items as cost, size, mechanical make-up, and suitability of the books under consideration.

Restrictions for Membership.—There are no uniform restrictions as to the membership of the adopting bodies. The requirement that not more than one member shall be appointed from the same county or congressional district occurs several times, as do the requirements that members shall not be interested directly or indirectly in the adoptions, and that they be actively engaged in educational work in the state. The state superintendent is usually a member of the adopting body and frequently the executive officer.

B. SCOPE AND EFFECT

Area of Uniformity.—Table 3 shows that twenty-five states have state uniformity laws, five have county uniformity, and seventeen have local adoptions. One state, Iowa, has optional county or local uniformity, but most of the counties in that state have adopted county uniformity by popular vote, and it is, therefore, classed with the county-uniformity states. North Carolina has state uniformity for elementary textbooks and county uniformity for high school books.

Grades Affected.—Nine of the twenty-five uniformity states have uniformity only for elementary textbooks, while sixteen states require uniformity of textbooks for all grades. Table 5 shows which states require complete uniformity and which require uniformity in only the elementary grades.

Of the county-uniformity states, Wisconsin requires uniformity only in the elementary grades. All of the others require complete uniformity.

Degree of Prescription.—Uniformity is generally interpreted to mean a single list of books, usually one book for each subject taught in each grade. In the case of readers it is customary to adopt both "basal" and "co-basal" books. This is especially true for the lower grades. In Delaware the state board of education prescribes a multiple list of books from which special districts may adopt for themselves; other districts are limited to a single list. In Maryland the matter of a single list or a multiple list is left to the county superintendent of each

TABLE 5

THE 25 UNIFORMITY STATES GROUPED ACCORDING TO DEGREE OF UNIFORMITY

Complete Uniformity	Uniformity Only in Elementary Grades
Alabama	Arizona
Delaware	Arkansas
Florida	California
Indiana	Georgia
Kansas	Idaho
Kentucky	Montana
Louisiana	Nevada
Mississippi	New Mexico
North Carolina	West Virginia
Oklahoma	
Oregon	
South Carolina	
Tennessee	
Texas	
Utah	
Virginia	

county. In Louisiana and Utah either a single or a multiple list may be prescribed by the adopting bodies of those states. In the other uniformity states a single list is prescribed for the elementary grades.

A few states have provided multiple lists for high school textbooks. Indiana provides a multiple list for certain high school subjects and a single list for certain others. Mississippi directs its adopting body for high school books to arrange a program of studies for each type of high school in the state and to adopt suitable books to fit the needs of their respective programs. Tennessee prescribes a multiple list for all high schools, and Texas prescribes a multiple list for high schools of the first class. All other uniformity states prescribe single lists for their high schools.

In no state is there any specific provision for junior high school books. Arkansas exempts junior high school grades from the operation of its uniformity law where there is a well-defined junior high school organization, but in all other uniformity states, the textbook laws do not recognize the junior high school as a distinct type. Under the law junior high schools must use the books adopted for elementary and high schools.

Seven of the non-uniformity states prescribe an "open list" from which local districts may make adoptions. The "open list" appears to be a method of regulating the price of textbooks rather than a selective process. Publishers who wish to do business in an "open list" state are usually required to furnish to the state superintendent samples of their books and to file with him a price schedule which sets forth the lowest price at which his books are sold elsewhere in the United States. The publisher must agree to sell his books in an "open list" state at prices no higher than he charges in other states. He is required to file a suitable bond, and penalties are provided for violation. A fee is usually charged for each book filed, to cover the cost of listing. Since there are no restrictions on the number or character of books which may be listed, the "open list" device operates only to regulate prices.

Term of Adoption.—The term of years for which books are adopted in the several states varies from three years to ten years, with five years as the most common term. Table 6 shows the number of states which have each adoption period.

TABLE 6

THE TERM OF YEARS FOR WHICH ADOPTIONS ARE MADE

Term of Adoption	Number of States
Indefinite	10 States
3 years	2 States
4 years	3 States
5 years	21 States
6 years	9 States
8 years	2 States
10 years	1 State

In most states books may be re-adopted at the end of the stated period if the adopting body considers it advisable. In most of the uniformity states the law provides that only a specified proportion of the textbooks may be changed in any one year.

Revision and Dropping.—Five states have made specific provisions for periodic revision of adopted textbooks, and seven states have laws which permit them to drop from the list adopted books which prove to be unsatisfactory after trial.

Supplementary Books.—Twenty-one states have made definite provisions for supplementary books, which usually consist of supplementary readers. They commonly provide that supplementary books may not be used to the exclusion of the basal texts.

Price Regulations.—Thirty-eight states have laws regulating the prices of textbooks. The usual provision in any given state is to the effect that no higher prices may be charged in that state than are charged elsewhere in the United States, taking into consideration cost of shipping and dealers' commission. It is usually provided also that when an adopted book is sold at a lower price in any state, then the contract price in the given state must be lowered to the same price.

Exchange Regulations.—Thirty states have made specific provisions for regulating the prices at which adopted books may be exchanged for more recently adopted books. The exchange period is usually limited to one year from the date of adoption of the new series.

Most uniformity states require that the retail price and the exchange price be printed on the outside covers of the adopted books.

Exemptions.—Fifteen states exempt from their uniformity laws cities and districts of certain specific sizes or classes. Mississippi provides that any school district may adopt its own high school books on a majority vote of the local board.

C. ADMINISTRATIVE PROCEDURES AND LEGAL SAFEGUARDS

Duties and Powers of Adopting Bodies.—To insure the operation of textbook laws in accordance with the intentions of the law-making bodies, the adopting bodies of the several states are usually given large discretionary powers to enforce the provisions of these laws. Even in the states where no specific authority is granted, such authority is implicit in the general powers of the adopting bodies.

As is shown in Table 3, in ten states the adopting bodies are given full power to make all rules necessary to carry out the provisions of the law. Such rules have the force of law. In addition to the general powers granted such bodies a number of states have made additional provisions to safeguard the operation of their textbook laws. Twenty states have provided that the adopting body must advertise for sealed bids. They are generally required to advertise in some one or more newspapers published in the state, and, in addition, to notify by letter publishers who may be interested. Such advertisements or notices must give full information concerning the books to be considered for adoption, the terms and form in which the bid must be made, the time and place when bids will be open, and such other detailed information as may be necessary to insure fair competition.

Adopting bodies are not bound to accept lowest prices. They are expected to consider the item of price, but they are not controlled by it. They usually have the right to reject any or all bids and to call for new bids, if in their judgment such action seems advisable.

Deposits.—Sixteen states specifically require a deposit in some stipulated amount to accompany bids, to insure execution of the bond and the contract if the bids are accepted. Such deposits are returned to the bidders if their bids are rejected, or when they have made bonds and signed contracts, if their bids are accepted.

Surety Bonds.—In twenty-nine states successful bidders are required by law to file surety bonds varying in amount from $1,000 to $50,000, the exact amount to be determined by the adopting body in the light of the number or value of the books adopted. These bonds all are conditioned on the full and faithful performance of the provisions of the contract by the publisher. It is usually provided that such bonds shall not be exhausted by a single recovery but may be sued upon from time to time as the circumstances may warrant. Such bonds run to the state and they must be approved by the attorney-general of the state. Suit for violation of the provisions of the contract is brought by the attorney-general in the name of the state.

Efforts to Influence Adoptions.—Eighteen states have made specific provisions against efforts on the part of publishers to influence adoptions, and twelve states have specific provisions against combinations of publishers in restraint of free competition. In North Carolina and Florida the names of the members of the subcommittee appointed to select textbooks are not divulged until they meet to make up their report. Apparently it was expected that this provision of the law would operate to curtail the efforts of publishers to influence adoptions. In Texas the law permits only the author, the publisher, or a bona fide permanent and regular employee of the publisher to appear before the textbook commission on behalf of any book under consideration. Penalties are provided for violations of the provision of the law, usually as for a misdemeanor, with fines in specified amounts for violations.

Depositories.—Nineteen states provide specifically for textbook depositories, to be maintained jointly or separately by the contracting publishers. In the other states which have uniformity laws the adopting body designates depositories, usually at least one in each county and one or more in each city. Under the latter plan local book dealers order adopted books direct from the publisher. They are permitted under the law to sell such books at retail prices ten to fifteen per cent above the wholesale price. A penalty, usually as for a misdemeanor, is provided for overcharging.

Adopting bodies are generally authorized to prescribe rules governing the distribution of adopted textbooks within the state. In Florida textbooks are shipped from the state school book depository to the several county superintendents, who redistribute them to the schools within the county. At the close of the school term the books are collected and brought back to the county superintendent's office, to be redistributed at the beginning of the next term of school.

Fumigation.—In three states (Arizona, Florida, and Idaho) the law requires fumigation of used books before they are reissued, but it is evident that this feature of the law is not strictly enforced. In Florida the state superintendent reports that he has heard of only one or two instances in the state where fumigation has been attempted. Competent health authorities have given him written opinions to the effect that fumigation is practically useless. In any event, no effort is made to enforce this provision of the law in Florida.

D. FREE TEXTBOOKS

Table 3 shows that only five of the forty-eight states are without laws relating to free textbooks. Twenty states require that free books be furnished either for the elementary grades or for all grades, and twenty-three states specifically permit local districts or counties to spend public school funds to supply free textbooks. In Table 7, which is derived from Table 3, the states are listed as having either mandatory or permissive free textbook laws. This table also shows for each state what grades are affected and the source of the funds.

TABLE 7

STATUS OF FREE TEXTBOOK LAWS IN ALL STATES HAVING SUCH LAWS

MANDATORY	ELEM. SCHOOL GRADES	ALL GRADES	SOURCE OF FUNDS	PERMISSIVE	ELEM. SCHOOL GRADES	ALL GRADES	SOURCE OF FUNDS
Arizona	x	..	State	Alabama	x	..	Local[4]
California	..	x	State[2]	Arkansas	x	..	Local
Delaware	..	x	State	Colorado	..	x	Local
Florida	x	..	State	Connecticut	..	x	Local
Maine	..	x	Local	Georgia	..	x	Local
Maryland	..	x	State	Idaho	..	x	Local
Massachusetts	..	x	Local	Illinois	..	x	Local
Montana	..	x	Local	Iowa	..	x	Local
Nebraska	..	x	Local	Kansas	..	x	Local
Nevada	x	..	State	Michigan	..	x	Local
New Hampshire	..	x	Local	Minnesota	..	x	Local
New Jersey	..	x	Local	Mississippi	..	x	Local
New Mexico	x	..	State	Missouri	x	..	Local[4]
Pennsylvania	..	x	Local	New York	..	x	Local
Rhode Island	..	x	Local	N. Carolina	..	x	Local
South Dakota	..	x	Local	N. Dakota	..	x	Local
Texas	..	x	State	Ohio	..	x	Local
Utah	x	..	Local	Oklahoma	..	x	Local
Vermont[1]	x	..	Local	Tennessee[3]	..	x	Local
Wyoming	..	x	Local	Virginia	..	x	Local
				Washington	..	x	Local
				W. Virginia	..	x	Local
				Wisconsin	..	x	Local

[1] Permissive for high school grades.
[2] For elementary grades only; local districts pay for high school books.
[3] By special legislation.
[4] With some state aid.

Table 7 shows that fourteen of the twenty states in which free textbooks are mandatory require all textbooks to be furnished free, while six other states require only the elementary grades to be furnished with free textbooks. Eight of these states pay for free textbooks out of state funds. In the other twelve states local communities or counties must pay for textbooks out of local or county funds, depending on the adopting unit.

Of the twenty-three states having permissive free textbook laws, only three limit free books to the elementary grades. In the other twenty states free textbooks may be supplied in all grades. In this group of states books are paid for out of local funds, or out of county funds if the county is the adopting unit.

Free textbooks are free only in the sense that they are loaned without charge to school pupils. The books usually remain the property of the state, the county, or the district, as the case may be, and they must be returned or accounted for at the close of the school year. These books are reissued each year until they are no longer serviceable. Usually pupils, or their parents, are required to pay for lost books or books damaged beyond ordinary wear and tear.

Pupils are not required to use free textbooks if they prefer to purchase their own books. This provision is made, presumably, to meet some of the objections to free textbooks, which will be developed in a later chapter of this study.

E. STATE PRINTED TEXTBOOKS

Five states (California, Kansas, Oklahoma, South Dakota, and Tennessee) have laws under which textbooks are or may be printed by the state, but only California and Kansas have actually undertaken the task. California began printing her own textbooks in 1884 by constitutional amendment. Kansas followed in 1913. Various other states have investigated the matter through special commissions appointed by their legislative bodies, but their reports have not been favorable to the plan.

That California's experience has not been wholly satisfactory is indicated in an article[1] prepared by a former state superintendent of public instruction at the request of the United States Commissioner of Education. Summarizing the twenty-year period from 1883 to 1903, he characterizes it as

> a time of contention, strife and abuse, and very disquieting to those who were responsible for the enterprise [state printing of textbooks]. The newness of the scheme shocked people's minds and roused their antagonism. The mechanical difficulties to be overcome were innumerable. Some editions were badly bound. Some books were poorly written. Every

[1] U. S. Bureau of Education, Bulletin, 1915, No. 36, pp. 57-63. Washington, D. C.

teacher preferred to use some favorite textbook. There were hundreds of book dealers in the state who were deprived of the profits of retailing books. The great publishing houses naturally opposed the whole idea of state publication. The leading educators almost universally followed suit. Institutes, clubs, and associations condemned it. No educational gathering was complete that did not take a fall out of the state textbooks. Undoubtedly, if it had not been planted deep in the constitution itself, state publication would have gone by the board during this period.

In 1903 the attorney-general of the state held that

> although the books themselves must be manufactured at the state printing office, there was nothing in the constitution that required local authorship, nothing to prevent the state board from leasing or buying copyrights and plates of books already published for the use of the state printer.

This construction was hailed as a godsend. Although the plan of leasing plates from commercial publishers did, to some extent, improve the situation, there was still considerable public criticism.

> The chief storm center at this time was the cost of the books to the children, alleged to be caused by their frequent change, although the law requiring no change in less than four years and no book contract for less than four years was strictly adhered to. Several of the books stood unchanged from a dozen to a score of years. However, it was found that when a book had been in use for four years so many people were fighting it that it must needs be changed. During the latter part of this period determined efforts were made to lower the cost. The publishers very generally entered into competition and the royalties were reduced from about 20 per cent to about 15 per cent of the list price. No headway, however, could be made in lowering the manufacturing cost. In general, the price to the children was somewhat below the publisher's list price for the same book, and the book in most cases was specially adapted to California use by changes and supplements in the plates.

Finally in 1912 a constitutional amendment was passed which provided that

> The state board may cause such textbooks, when adopted, to be printed and published by the superintendent of state printing at the state printing office, and wherever and however such textbooks may be printed and published they shall be furnished and distributed by the state free of cost or any charge whatever to all children attending the day and evening elementary schools of the state under such conditions as the legislature shall prescribe.

Cubberley condemns the plan of state publication of textbooks in most vigorous terms. In his *State School Administration,*[2] he

[2] Cubberley, E. P. *State School Administration,* Chap. XXI. Houghton Mifflin, 1927.

discusses California's experience in detail, and he concludes with the statement that

> The unbiased judgment of those who have examined the question most carefully is that there is no educational or business reason why any state should attempt it; all arguments for the plan, such as the home-industry idea rests on grounds other than these.

In California, state publishing is limited to elementary textbooks, but in Kansas the state is authorized to publish both elementary and high school books. As a matter of fact, Kansas has published only four high school textbooks (one in geometry, two in algebra, and one in English).

CHAPTER III

TEXTBOOK LEGISLATION IN FLORIDA

Prior to 1899 textbook legislation in Florida, generally speaking, was rather ineffective. As early as 1875 the state board of education adopted a uniform series of textbooks for the state, but the action had no legal basis and it was generally ignored. Various succeeding state superintendents recommended either state or county uniformity with long-term adoptions, but apparently no action was taken by the legislature until 1883.

In 1883 the legislature passed an act requiring county uniformity within the several counties for a term of five years. This law seems to have met with general approval. Various county superintendents reported to the state superintendent in their annual reports that they had adopted uniform textbooks in their respective counties, and that the adopted books were generally satisfactory.

But by 1897 some doubt seems to have arisen in the minds of the county superintendents as to the wisdom of the policy of county uniformity. During the state convention of county superintendents in 1897, one of the topics discussed was the uniformity question. The question as proposed was as follows: "Is uniformity to any extent preferable? to what extent? is it desirable for the whole state?" Several county superintendents spoke on the topic, and one of them summed up the situation since the enactment of the law of 1883. He said [1] in part:

> The experience is that we need some uniformity. For a great many years it was the practice in this state to allow the teacher of a school to introduce and use just such books as suited his fancy. The course of study was his own creation, the textbooks after his own notion. Changing the teacher necessitated changing books, as well as the courses of study. Laws were made requiring that we have uniformity in our counties. These adoptions were first made in 1883, supposedly for a five-year period, and it has not changed in practice since. Most counties have made uniform adoptions since then on the five-year plan. There are some counties now

[1] *Florida School Report,* 1896-98, p. 465.

breaking away from this, having heard that there was no real law requiring it. Quite a number of counties, according to my information, have not entered into another contract with any book company for any length of time.

He then proceeded to discuss the question, showing the advantages of county uniformity over state uniformity.

Other speakers argued in favor of state uniformity and still others in favor of or against free textbooks. At the end of the convention a resolution was offered and passed, 19 to 1, as follows:

Resolved, That state uniformity of textbooks is unwise, non-progressive and undemocratic; that county uniformity is desirable, and it is hereby recommended that the next legislature enact such laws as will legalize this plan; provide for the selection, adoption, purchase, and sale of books by county school authorities, and protect pupils and patrons.

The state superintendent agreed with the point of view expressed in this resolution and recommended to the legislature that a county uniformity law be passed. In his recommendation he says:

The state is entirely without any law upon the subject, since the law of 1893[2] was left out in the codification of the Revised Statutes.

The next legislature passed the act as recommended, with the proviso that the adoption of the system should be gradual but that it must be consummated by July 1, 1901.

Although the question of free textbooks had been discussed at one of the state conventions of county superintendents, it was still largely an academic matter. Four counties had adopted the free textbook plan prior to 1900. Hernando county was the first (1891); Osceola and Brevard counties followed in 1896; and Citrus county in 1898. The annual reports made by the county superintendents to the state superintendent indicate that the plan was generally satisfactory. Textbooks were more abundant and they were supplied more promptly at the opening of the school term. The cost was less, attendance was greatly increased, and the books were better kept and more carefully handled.

Soon after the adoption of the county uniformity law in 1899,

[2] Since no uniformity law was enacted in 1893, it seems probable that the date mentioned was intended for 1883.

the friends of state-wide uniformity began agitating. They argued that everything that could be said in favor of county uniformity could be said for state uniformity with even more force; that under county uniformity there was considerable loss on textbooks when families moved from one county to another; that many county boards were incompetent to select the best books; and that books would be cheaper under state uniformity.

The state superintendent, in his report for the biennium ending June 30, 1900, recommended that no change be made in the textbook law. He thought that "too much risk is attended with so mammoth a scheme when a wrong act or error is as far-reaching in consequence as to affect the whole state." In his report for the biennium ending June 30, 1902, he says: [3]

> It is difficult to understand why the perennially recurring agitation for state uniformity of textbooks should receive any consideration at the hands of the legislature. It is a most undemocratic and offensive proposition to mold all the minds of the state by means of the same textbooks, and it passes my comprehension how it is expected to crush a trust by creating a state monopoly. It appears that if a monopoly is to exist the so-called trust would be quite sure to reap the lion's share of the advantage. As a matter of fact, however, if there is any trust involved in the question, a careful investigation will readily show that it is a case of a trust trying to fight a trust, and using the state as a cat's paw, with no reference to the interests of the cat. There is abundant evidence to show that there is a combination of book companies who did not succeed in making contracts with the county boards in 1901 and, being unwilling to wait until the expiration of the present contracts in 1906, and then take even chances, have combined to overthrow the present law and put the state to the expense of changing textbooks throughout, in order to secure business where they have heretofore failed. It is regretted also that an unworthy appeal has been made to sectionalism, and one company has been pushed forward as a Southern textbook publisher in the hope of catching prejudiced and unwary legislators. It is not believed that the Florida legislature will be deceived in this matter as some others have been.
>
> My investigations have tended clearly to show that there is no advantage in state uniformity comparable to the disadvantages and dangers. It is the opinion of the educational experts, including the United States Commissioner of Education and practically all the educators of this state and leaders in educational thought elsewhere, who have expressed themselves upon it, that it is an unwise measure. I am fully convinced that any cheapening in price will be fully offset by cheapening in quality. This has been the experience of other states and Florida cannot hope to fare better.

[3] *Florida School Report, 1902,* p. 426.

In the same report he discusses free textbooks as follows:

> This subject is mentioned neither to commend nor to oppose the system, provided the cost of the books is met by a special tax levy. But with an average school term in the state of only 94 days, I seriously question the wisdom of further reducing this ruinously short term for the benefits of free books or any other desirable good. The reduction in term at the lowest estimate would average 10 days—considerably more in some counties, if the cost of books is to be taken from present inadequate funds.
>
> The inauguration of the system must cost the state not less than $150,000, unless the books now owned by pupils are donated; after that about $50,000 a year, provided the system is guarded in every county against needless waste by having men of good business management to look carefully after the distribution and gathering up of the books.
>
> Two or three of the smaller counties of the state have experimented with the system and pronounce the results most satisfactory. It unquestionably has its advantages, and there is an appreciable gain in the aggregate results of a short school term, growing out of furnishing every child with books on the first day of school and the very grade of book that it ought to use.
>
> Whether or not I would favor free textbooks depends almost wholly upon the size of the school fund, whether the maximum county levy is to be raised, and the school term, now far too short, is to be still further shortened.
>
> To be frank, I am not enthusiastic in advocacy of the system with present outlook for funds.

Despite the attitude of the state superintendent, the friends of state uniformity of textbooks continued to agitate the question, and apparently with some success so far as winning adherents to their cause was concerned. In his report for the biennium ending June 30, 1904, the state superintendent included reports from the several county superintendents. Among other topics upon which they were asked to report were the topics of state uniformity versus county uniformity of textbooks and free textbooks. Their replies,[4] summarized, were as follows:

For State uniformity	14
For County uniformity	19
For Free textbooks	8
Against Free textbooks	25

Twelve counties either failed to report at all or neglected to comment on these topics.

When it is recalled that in 1897 a resolution favoring county

[4] *Florida School Report, 1902-06*, pp. 251-365.

uniformity over state uniformity was passed at the state convention of county superintendents by a vote of 19 to 1, it is evident that the movement for state uniformity had gained ground.

Bills were introduced in each succeeding legislature to change county uniformity to state uniformity, but without immediate results other than to keep the issue alive. County superintendents continued to be divided on the question, as is shown in their annual reports to the state superintendent.

In September, 1910, the governor appointed a Committee on the Revision and Codification of the School Laws of the State of Florida. This committee, of which the state superintendent was chairman, recommended that the county uniformity law be continued and that certain amendments be made to insure to each county the lowest obtainable prices. The report of this committee was dated March 20, 1911. In spite of this recommendation, the state legislature passed a state uniformity law in May of the same year. (Acts of 1911—Chapter 6178.)

This law provided that the Board of Commissioners of State Institutions should constitute a state textbook commission, with authority to adopt a uniform series of textbooks for the public schools of the state for a term of five years. Although the law did not specifically exempt high schools, the branches for which specific provision was made were the usual elementary school subjects. It was provided that any school might adopt books of its own choosing for higher branches of study than those specified.

A subcommission was provided under the law, which subcommission was composed of four county superintendents and five teachers, all appointed by the governor.

Specimen copies of textbooks under consideration were referred to the subcommission, which made a report upon the merits of each book, "irrespective of price, taking into consideration the subject matter, the printing, the material, the mechanical qualities, and the general suitability and desirability of the books for the purposes for which they were desired and intended." The books so reported upon were ranked in order of merit and books which were regarded as unsuitable were so designated. The report was sealed and kept secret until it was opened in executive session of the commission.

Members of the subcommission were appointed to serve for

four years. Each member was required to take an oath to the effect that he was not related in any way to any member of the board of commissions of state institutions, that he had not been previously employed by any textbook publisher in any capacity, and that he would carefully and conscientiously examine all books submitted to him and make a true report thereon.

The textbook commission was also required to examine the textbooks as well as to receive and consider the report of the subcommittee, taking into consideration the price factor. The final selection was made by the state textbook commission. If it chose to ignore the recommendations of the subcommittee it was free to do so.

The textbook commission was required to organize, with the governor as ex-officio president and the superintendent of public instruction as secretary. The law required advertising for sealed bids, the latter to be for furnishing books for five years and no longer. A deposit of not less than $500 and not more than $2,500 was to accompany each bid to insure execution of the contract and bond in the case of successful bidders. Deposits of unsuccessful bidders were returned.

After the commission had made a selection of books for adoption, contracts were drawn up which provided that all books furnished under it should be equal in all respects to the samples submitted; that the contract price and the exchange price should be printed plainly on the back of each book; and that the prices named in the contract should be as low as the prices at which the same books were sold anywhere else in the United States. The law also provided that not more than ten per cent of the whole number of adopted books could be changed in any one year, and publishers of books which were not changed were required to renew contracts for the next adoption period at prices as low as those previously quoted. It was also provided that publishers who might secure contracts should exchange new books for old books, allowing for the old books fifty per cent of the contract price of the new books.

The commission reserved the right to reject any or all bids and to re-advertise for new bids in case it saw fit to do so.

Contractors were required to maintain not less than one nor more than twelve distributing agencies in each county, as the commission might deem advisable. The commission was authorized to make any necessary regulations not contrary to the law to secure the prompt and faithful performance of all contracts.

Counties which were already under contract were excluded from the provision of the law until existing contracts should expire, but no new contracts were permitted.

It was provided that only the state-adopted books should be used after the passage of this act, and heavy penalties were provided for violations of it.

The law as enacted was not wholly satisfactory, apparently, although in his report for the biennium ending June 30, 1914, the state superintendent recommended that the law be left intact. He went on to say [5] that

> it was a mistake that all the counties were not required to adopt the prescribed books at the same time and that a depository was not demanded for the state.

In the same report a number of county superintendents complained that local book dealers had failed to lay in sufficient stocks of books, because their margin of profit was so small, and as a result many children had been without books for the entire school term.

During the state convention of county superintendents held that year (1914) one of the topics discussed had to do with difficulties in securing textbooks, their causes and suggested remedies. The committee of the commission on resolutions and legislation recommended an amendment to the textbook law abolishing the textbook commission and placing entire authority to select and adopt books under the subcommission, but nothing was done about the matter.

In 1915 the legislature, with the consent of the publishers, extended the adoption period to 1917 in an effort to bring about state uniformity without working a hardship on certain counties which had recently made adoptions. In 1917 the legislature again extended the original adoption period to 1919.

In the same year (1917) the original state uniformity law was amended to include high school textbooks; to make the subcommission more nearly representative of the different grade levels; and to provide for a state school book depository.

[5] *Florida School Report, 1912-14*, p. 54.

These changes in the law seemed to remove most of the causes for complaint. In the 1918 biennial report of the state superintendent of public instruction the county superintendents were practically unanimous in their approval of the law. Some of the adopted books were not wholly satisfactory, but in the main there was little opposition to the textbook law or to its operation. Sentiment with reference to free textbooks was still about equally divided.

In his report for 1920 the state superintendent recommended that the original law be further amended, or that an entirely new law be passed. He thought the date of adopting books should come earlier in the year than July 1, and that the entire matter of adoptions should be left largely to the state textbook commission, thereby eliminating much useless detail from the law.

Apparently his recommendations were approved by the legislature. In 1921 a new textbook law was passed. It is the law now in force so far as uniformity is concerned. It provides for adoption terms of eight years instead of five, for both elementary and high school books. The state textbook commission is authorized to make all needful regulations governing adoption procedure.

This law provides a subcommission, composed of "seven prominent educators engaged in school work in the state," appointed by the governor on recommendation of the state superintendent of public instruction. As in the previous law, the membership of the committee, which serves for only one adoption, is kept secret until it meets at the capitol to begin its duties.

The subcommission is required to examine the various books under consideration and to rank them in order of merit down to its fifth choice, giving a brief report on the merits or demerits of each book. This report, which is delivered to the state textbook commission, is kept secret until the commission meets to adopt books, after which adoption the report is filed with the state superintendent and is available for public inspection.

The state textbook commission is also required to examine the books to be adopted and to "adopt such books as will, in its own best judgment, best serve the ends desired."

The law requires the completion of the adoption on or before March 1, in order that contractors may have ample time in which to supply books by July 1—the beginning of the school year.

Each contractor or the several contractors combined are required to establish and maintain a book depository within the state in such place as the textbook commission may designate, and to maintain one or more agencies in each county for convenient and speedy distribution of books.

Heavy penalties are provided for violations of the law.

The new law remedied many of the defects of the earlier law but apparently not all of them. In the state superintendent's biennial report for 1922, several county superintendents reported that they had been unable to get enough textbooks for their needs. At the state conference of county superintendents held in 1922 it was brought out that local book dealers were allowed a gross profit of only ten per cent, and that such a small margin of profit was insufficient to warrant dealers in stocking textbooks and assuming risks incidental to the business. It was suggested that local dealers be allowed a gross profit of 15 to 20 per cent. Opinion on the question of free textbooks was still divided, although one or two more counties had adopted the free book plan.

In 1925 a law was enacted to provide for the furnishing of free textbooks in the first six grades of all the public schools of Florida, at the expense of the state. This law became effective on July 1, 1926.

The law provides that each county superintendent shall make requisition on the state superintendent of public instruction for such books as may be necessary to supply the pupils in the first six grades of the public schools of the county. The state superintendent then orders all necessary books from the publishers, to be shipped direct to the county superintendents. The publisher prepares duplicate invoices, one of which is sent to the county superintendent and the other to the state superintendent. The county superintendent checks the books received with the invoice therefor and if it is correct sends the approved invoice to the state superintendent, who presents it to the state school book commission. After approval by the latter body the invoice is delivered to the state controller, who pays it out of the state textbook fund. A special tax of three-fourths of one mill is levied against all assessable property within the state for the purpose of providing the textbook fund.

The county superintendent delivers to the principal or teacher of each school in the county the required number of books and takes a receipt therefor. The teacher distributes the books to the pupils and takes their receipt or the receipt of their parents or guardians. At the close of the school year, the process is reversed, the pupil returning the books to the teacher and the teacher to county superintendent. Pupils must pay for lost books or books unnecessarily damaged.

The county superintendent is required to fumigate all used books before they are re-issued. Failure to do so is a misdemeanor and is punishable as such.

It is provided also that any pupil who may choose to do so may purchase and own any of the adopted books, at the contract price.

Since this law has been in operation only one and one-half years its advantages and disadvantages are not fully developed.

ATTITUDES OF TEACHERS

In order to find out how satisfactory the present law is from the standpoint of the teachers in the state a questionnaire was sent to approximately one thousand teachers, selected by the method of random sampling from representative schools in ten representative counties. Care was taken to secure returns from the various types and classes of schools in each county. The questionnaire form is reproduced on page 38.

Replies were received from 732 elementary teachers, from 89 junior high school teachers, and from 95 senior high school teachers. The results were tabulated for each county and by classes of schools within each county. No significant differences were noted between rural schools and city schools within counties, and no significant differences were noted between different counties. While the contention that different classes of schools need different kinds of books is not borne out by the returns from this questionnaire, it is possible that the books now in use are not any better adapted to one class of school than they are to another.

Table 8, which is a composite tabulation of all the returns

for the elementary schools, indicates that certain adopted books are much less satisfactory than certain other adopted books. The reasons given for dissatisfaction with most of the adopted books cover the entire range of possibilities offered by the questionnaire, but for certain books there is a decided tendency for certain reasons to be given much more frequently than others. For example, the adopted readers are unsatisfactory to 190

EDUCATIONAL SURVEY MEASUREMENT PROGRAM

THE INSTITUTE OF EDUCATIONAL RESEARCH DIVISION OF FIELD STUDIES

TEACHERS COLLEGE, COLUMBIA UNIVERSITY

REPORT ON STATE-ADOPTED TEXTBOOKS

County .... School .... Date......

Teacher .... Grade or Subject ....

Total Teaching Experience .... years. Experience in this Grade .... years

---

Please place a check mark (√) to the right of each of the state-adopted books which you find unsatisfactory, and also the number or numbers of the reasons for your dissatisfaction. Do not check satisfactory books.

ADOPTED BOOKS

Elementary Schools

1. Readers
2. Arithmetic
3. Speller
4. Grammar or Language
5. Physiology and Hygiene
6. History
7. Geography
8. Music
9. Supplementary Books
10. ....
11. ....
12. ....

High School

(Write in the name of any unsatisfactory book)

1. ....
2. ....
3. ....
4. ....

REASONS FOR DISSATISFACTION

1. Too difficult for pupils
2. Too easy for pupils
3. Not up to date
4. Not interesting to pupils
5. Hard to teach
6. Not well planned
7. Does not promote growth
8. Unsuitable method
9. Unsatisfactory to patrons
10. Size of type
11. Quality of paper
12. Binding
13. Illustrations
14. Insufficient supply
15. Delay in receiving supply
16. Clerical work in accounting
17. Fumigation requirements
18. Dirty books
19. ....
20. ....
21. ....
22. ....

For other comments, use the back of this sheet

teachers because they are too difficult (for beginners). The spellers are unsatisfactory to 74 teachers because they are not up to date (in method of word selection). The text in language and grammar is not interesting to the pupils in the judgment of 80 teachers, while to 96 teachers this text seems poorly planned. Clerical duties connected with free textbooks make the whole plan objectionable to 68 teachers and the dirtiness of books is unsatisfactory to 70 teachers. Of the entire group of 732 teachers only 167 found all of the adopted books satisfactory.

In the case of textbooks reported on by junior high school teachers, the returns were generally made in the form of comments on the adopted books. Only two teachers of the 89 who filled out the questionnaire found the books which they were

TABLE 8

NUMBER OF TEACHERS * WHO FOUND EACH OF THE ADOPTED BOOKS UNSATISFACTORY AND FOR WHAT REASONS

REASON FOR DISSATISFACTION	READERS	ARITHMETIC	SPELLER	GRAMMAR AND LANGUAGE	PHYSIOLOGY AND HYGIENE	HISTORY	GEOGRAPHY	MUSIC	SUPPLEMENTARY READERS	ALL FREE TEXTBOOKS
1. Too difficult for pupils...	190	14	5	12	1	25	15	1	6	..
2. Too easy for pupils......	3	6	3	9	8	0	1	0	0	..
3. Not up to date..........	37	31	74	24	12	5	33	0	1	..
4. Not interesting to pupils.	75	18	34	80	4	7	38	0	1	..
5. Hard to teach...........	27	15	16	51	1	15	29	0	0	..
6. Not well planned........	40	67	67	96	7	13	25	1	0	..
7. Does not promote growth	12	6	17	24	2	6	13	0	0	..
8. Unsuitable method	14	13	46	18	5	4	20	3	0	..
9. Unsatisfactory to patrons.	1	1	0	0	0	0	2	0	0	..
10. Size of type............	6	0	0	0	1	3	4	0	0	..
11. Quality of paper.........	0	0	0	0	0	0	0	0	0	..
12. Binding	4	2	1	0	0	10	0	0	0	..
13. Illustrations	1	2	1	2	0	1	5	0	0	..
14. Insufficient supply	0	0	0	0	0	0	0	0	14	..
15. Delay in receiving supply	3	0	0	0	0	0	0	0	0	..
16. Clerical work in accounting	..	..	..	..	..	..	..	..	..	68
17. Fumigation requirements.	..	..	..	..	..	..	..	..	..	0
18. Dirty books	..	..	..	..	..	..	..	..	..	70
19. No dissatisfaction	..	..	..	..	..	..	..	..	..	167

* Reports were received from 732 teachers.

using reasonably satisfactory. A criticism which occurred frequently was that the adopted books were not designed for use in junior high school organizations.

Of the 95 high school teachers who made returns, 10 were satisfied with the textbooks they were using. The remaining 85 gave various reasons for their dissatisfaction, usually in considerable detail. One reason which was given frequently was that the adopted books were not of the latest editions published. For example, "the adopted text in general science is of the 1918 edition, although three later editions have been published." The textbook in algebra in one school was reported as being of the 1912 edition. In many instances textbooks were suggested which in the opinions of the reporting teachers would be more satisfactory than those now in use.

It is obvious that the results obtained from this questionnaire are not highly significant so far as particular textbooks are concerned. Judgments of individual teachers may have been influenced by various factors, such as amount of their professional training, years of experience in teaching, degree of preparation of pupils, or unconscious bias of one kind or another. It is worth noting, however, that only 180 teachers of the 916 who returned questionnaires report themselves as being satisfied with the adopted textbooks. Stated otherwise, four-fifths of the teachers who reported are finding one or more of the adopted textbooks unsatisfactory in one respect or another.

It is, of course, possible that as large a proportion of the teachers in the state or even a larger proportion, would be dissatisfied with any other single list of textbooks that might be adopted. Cause for discontent may be inherent in the plan of adopting a single list of textbooks for the entire state. A part of the dissatisfaction with the books now in use may arise out of the fact that the teachers themselves have had so little to do with the choosing of the textbooks which they must use. Whatever the reasons for dissatisfaction may be, any reasonable plan that offers a solution for the difficulty would seem worthy of careful consideration.

ATTITUDE OF COUNTY SUPERINTENDENTS

The foregoing section has had to do with the attitude of classroom teachers toward the textbooks now in use in the state. In order to discover the attitude of the county superintendents toward the present textbook law and its operation, a questionnaire was sent to each of the 67 county superintendents in the state.

TABLE 9

SUMMARY OF REPLIES RECEIVED FROM FIFTY-THREE COUNTY SUPERINTENDENTS IN RESPONSE TO QUESTIONNAIRE

Question	Reply		
	Yes	No	No Reply
1. Are the state-adopted books reasonably satisfactory for the elementary schools in your county?	45	8	0
For the junior high schools?	31	20	2
For the senior high schools?	41	11	1
2. In your opinion would better educational results be obtained if different sets of books were used in different classes of schools?			
In elementary grades?	13	39	1
In junior high school grades?	10	41	2
In senior high school grades?	10	42	1
3. Is the 8-year term of adoption too long?	33	19	1
4. Should the state be the unit of textbook uniformity for			
elementary schools?	48	1	4
junior high schools?	44	4	5
senior high schools?	47	1	5
5. Should the state be the unit of uniformity for courses of study for			
elementary schools?	46	3	4
junior high schools?	43	5	5
senior high schools?	46	3	4
6. Has school attendance improved since the adoption of the free textbook plan?	20	30	3
7. Does the free textbook plan increase clerical duties of teachers to an objectionable extent?	22	31	0
8. Under the free textbook plan does class work start more promptly at the beginning of the school term?	42	9	2
9. Are textbooks more soiled and unattractive under the free book plan than they were under private ownership?	21	30	2
10. Do parents or pupils object to using second-hand books?	33	20	0
11. Do you fumigate used books before reissue?	27	24	2
12. Are supplementary books satisfactory?	43	8	2
13. Should the free textbook plan be extended?	37	14	2
to include the 8th grade?	23	..	..
to include the 12th grade?	13	..	..

Table 9 is a summary of the fifty-three replies which were received in response to the questionnaire.

To most of the county superintendents the state-adopted books now in use in the elementary schools and high schools are reasonably satisfactory. Junior high school textbooks seem to be much less so. There is very little sentiment in favor of different lists of textbooks for different types and classes of schools. State uniformity of textbooks and state uniformity for courses of study are satisfactory, but the eight-year term of adoption seems entirely too long to most county superintendents. Five years is the term most frequently suggested. While the free textbook plan has not greatly improved attendance, in the opinion of most of those who reported, they are certain that class work gets started more promptly at the beginning of the school term. There is considerable objection on the part of teachers, principals, and county superintendents to the additional clerical duties imposed by the free textbook plan. Books are reported as being no more soiled and unattractive than they would be under private ownership. About two-thirds of the county superintendents who reported state that both parents and pupils object to the use of soiled books. In only twenty-seven of the fifty-three counties reporting are school books being fumigated. Supplementary readers seem satisfactory for the most part. There is a definite feeling that the free textbooks plan should be extended to include all elementary grades, and there is some feeling that free books should be furnished to all grades.

In this chapter the aim has been to trace the development of textbook legislation in Florida and to determine to some extent the attitude of those who are engaged in school work in the state toward the operation of the existing textbook laws. Knowledge of the past and present may be, in some measure, a guide for the future.

Dr. Carter Alexander, in an unpublished manuscript entitled "Standards for School Administration," proposes a set of criteria for evaluating policies and procedures with reference to given situations. Among others, he proposes the following:

Does it (the proposed policy) or will it meet the needs of the particular situation at the present time?

a. Is there sufficient conformity to the native characteristics, institutions, and economic conditions of the people in the area concerned?

b. **Is it in accordance with the facts of historical development both in the area (under consideration) and in the country at large?**

It is obvious that the answers to the foregoing questions must be in the affirmative if the proposed policy is to be considered sound.

For the purposes of this study the criterion proposed above may be accepted. That is, the textbook law which is to be proposed for Florida should take into consideration present needs, institutions, and economic conditions; and due consideration should be given to the historical development of textbook legislation in Florida and in the country at large.

The application of this criterion is general and not specific. Each item in the proposed law must be considered in the light of the standards here set up. No matter how ideal the proposed law may seem to be, and no matter how completely it may meet other specific criteria which may be set up, it must first of all conform to the requirement of the general criterion proposed above.

CHAPTER IV

ARGUMENTS FOR AND AGAINST UNIFORMITY AND FREE TEXTBOOKS

Much has been written about state uniformity of textbooks and free textbooks, but very little objective evidence has been offered for or against either proposition. The literature on these two topics consists almost wholly of arguments for and against state uniformity and free textbooks. The same arguments are used by many writers, so that, while the number of available references is fairly large, the number of arguments for or against either proposition is limited.

These arguments are presented herewith, summarized and classified, but without attempt to evaluate them or to weigh one against the other.

A. FOR STATE UNIFORMITY OF TEXTBOOKS

1

Under state uniformity textbooks cost less than they do under local adoptions. Adoptions are made for comparatively long terms and the publishers who secure the contracts can print their books in larger quantities without the risk of loss due to overprinting. Costs decrease as the size of editions increases.

Another reason for lower costs lies in the fact that the publishers who secure state contracts no longer have to maintain large forces of salesmen in that state. They can, and do, offer their books at lower prices than they could afford to do otherwise.

State textbook laws generally provide that no higher prices shall be charged for adopted textbooks in a given state than are charged in other states. Moreover, if prices are lowered on any adopted book in any other state, then the price must be lowered correspondingly in a given state. This provision insures the state against paying more for its textbooks than any other state pays.

Since a state adoption involves a large number of books over a comparatively long period, all publishers will compete vigorously to secure contracts, and to that end they will offer their books at lower prices than they would if competition were less necessary.

Rebuttal. The argument that textbooks are cheaper under state uniformity is unsound. Non-uniformity states which have "open lists" secure prices that are as low as prices quoted in uniformity states.

As a matter of fact, natural competition among publishers is sufficient to insure fair prices. No state has thought it necessary under normal conditions to try to regulate prices of other commodities, such as food or clothing.

2

Books selected by an adopting body consisting of persons appointed because of their professional qualifications are likely to be better than they would be if they were selected by local boards unfamiliar with educational problems.

Even if local boards would rely on the advice of their principals and teachers in adopting textbooks, good books would not be assured, because in many local districts, and especially in rural districts, principals and teachers are not professionally qualified to select the best books.

Textbooks should be selected only after careful and complete investigation of all offerings for a given subject. State commissions are better qualified and they have better facilities than local boards to do this work. Moreover, when each local district adopts its own books there is a large waste of energy due to duplications of effort in examining large numbers of books.

Rebuttal. Adopting bodies are commonly composed of about seven members. It is not reasonable to expect them to be sufficiently expert in all subjects and at all grade levels to make the best selection of textbooks. The law does not, apparently, contemplate professional advice from sources outside the membership of the adopting body; hence they must rely on themselves. Even when adopting bodies are selected so as to represent different grade levels, there can be only one or two members from each grade level. The actual selection of textbooks under such circumstances is, therefore, left to the judgment or prejudices of the one or two members who seem best qualified to make the selection.

3

When books are selected by a state adopting body, the teachers and other school officials throughout the state are relieved of the importunities of textbook salesmen. Textbook salesmen concern themselves less with local school politics, and teachers are not subjected to political and economic pressure as they frequently are under the plan of local adoptions. State adopting bodies are better able to withstand such pressure because they are hedged about with safeguards in the form of legal provisions to insure fair and open competition.

Rebuttal. State uniformity puts into the hands of a few the power to award contracts which determine whether or not any publisher may do business in a state. Publishers must, therefore, make every possible effort to insure the adoption of their own books. The temptation to resort to illegal practices is great. Political and social pressure and even bribery have been resorted to by publishers to secure adoptions.

4

The plan of state uniformity of textbooks avoids losses on books when families move from one school district to another. In the United States the population is constantly shifting. This is especially true of industrial and seasonal workers and artisans. Studies made by the United States Census Bureau show large interstate movements of people. A study made by the California Curriculum Study Commission on intra-state shifting of rural school pupils showed that less than one-third of the pupils who reach the eighth grade had continued in the same school system from the first grade and that 28.6 per cent had changed school systems four or more times. There is, and has been for several decades, a marked tendency on the part of the rural population to move to urban centers.

The pupil who moves from one district to another which uses different books loses the value of the book which he already owns.

Rebuttal. The argument that under state uniformity losses on books would be avoided when families move from one district to another has no point where textbooks are furnished free, as they are now furnished in most states. When a family moves from one district to another, textbooks are left behind since they are the property of the district or state under the free textbook plan.

5

The use of uniform textbooks throughout a state makes possible the formulation and adoption of a uniform minimum state course of study which can be enforced. The state cannot enforce a minimum course of study unless there is a large degree of uniformity as far as minimum essentials are concerned. The formulation of courses of study must be left to local districts under local adoption of textbooks because textbooks largely determine courses of study. Many local districts are not competent to formulate their own courses of study because of untrained teachers.

There should be a uniform minimum course of study throughout the state because of the constantly shifting school population. Without uniformity of courses of study pupils lose school standing—usually a half-grade—when they move from one school district to another. This would not be true if textbooks and courses of study were the same in all school districts within the state.

Rebuttal. The argument that uniform textbooks make possible a uniform course of study is based on the premise that a uniform course of study for the state is desirable. This is not true. It could be true only if all the children in the state were alike in their needs and their abilities. Within a given city, or even within a given school, uniform courses of study are undesirable and impracticable. Many schools have grouped their pupils into classes according to their abilities, and they have adapted their courses of study to the needs of each group.

B. AGAINST STATE UNIFORMITY OF TEXTBOOKS

1

Books which may be suitable for one locality may not be suitable for a different locality. School terms vary within a given state from six months to ten months. A book which is suitable for the longer school term cannot be covered by the school with the shorter term. The character and extent of supervision may vary from nothing at all in the rural school to highly expert supervision in city schools. Teachers may vary in ability, experience, and professional training from very little to very much. A book which would be suitable in the one instance could not be used successfully in the other.

But even if matters of supervision and length of term were disposed of, there would still remain the difference in the experiences of country children and city children. Granted that their fundamental educational needs may be the same, one of the largest assets a teacher has in the teaching process is the experience of the child. Textbooks are most effective as educational instruments when they are adapted to the experience of those who use them.

In cities where pupils are grouped according to ability, courses of study are ordinarily adapted to the needs and abilities of each group, whether slow-moving, fast-moving, or average. Textbooks should be different for each group with respect to wording, style, difficulty of material, and scope of treatment.

Uniformity of textbooks is even worse in junior and senior high schools. The latter types of schools are new and rapidly changing. In their very nature they must remain largely experimental and exploratory in character. The teacher in a small rural high school, usually inadequately supplied with library reference books and laboratory facilities, needs a textbook quite different from the one needed by the teacher in a large city high school with good library and laboratory equipment and highly specialized instruction.

2

State uniformity means comparatively long term adoptions—usually about five years in length. This provision of the law prevents the adoption of new and better textbooks which are constantly appearing. Scientific experimentation in education is going on all over the country. The results of such studies are being incorporated in textbooks. Schools should be free to select the best available books at all times. Under long-term adoptions this would not be possible.

3

Too much state control stifles individual enterprise and initiative. Most of the significant contributions to educational theory and practice have come from individuals who have been free to experiment. Such contributions could not have been made under a system providing uniform courses of study and uniform textbooks.

While education is a function of the state, and while the state must accept responsibility for a minimum educational program, it is fundamental to the American plan of government to delegate to the local community all responsibility which it is capable of administering effectively. Where local communities are not competent to make good courses of study and to select appropriate textbooks, the remedy should be sought in a more effective administrative and supervisory unit—not in state control.

C. FOR FREE TEXTBOOKS

1

In American schools textbooks are as essential as teachers or school buildings. In a system of free public schools there is no more reason why a child should furnish his own books than why he should pay his own share of the teacher's salary or the fuel bill or the janitor's wages. Textbooks are the tools the child uses in his school work. If he goes to school he must have textbooks. He would have no use or very little use for them otherwise. Public education cannot be said to be free so long as this essential part of the machinery is not furnished without cost to the pupil. Precisely the same arguments that are made for free public schools can be offered in favor of free textbooks, since the textbook, rightly considered, is a part of the school.

Not only is education free; it is compulsory within limits in every state in the Union. Compulsory education can be effective only when the necessary educational machinery is provided. Textbooks are a part of the necessary educational machinery. Compulsory school attendance goes hand in hand with free schools, including free teachers, free fuel, free janitors, free instructional supplies, and free textbooks.

2

The provision of free textbooks eliminates the delay in beginning a school term due to the slowness of parents in furnishing their children with necessary textbooks. In some cases parents may not be financially able to buy the necessary textbooks for several weeks after school opens; in other cases, particularly in rural districts, it may be inconvenient or difficult to reach the nearest school bookstore. Very little can be accomplished in the way of class instruction until all pupils have access to the necessary textbooks. Delays in getting started are serious under any circumstances, but they are especially serious in rural districts where the terms are usually shortest and where the delay in getting started is usually longest.

3

When textbooks are furnished free to all children, problems growing out of dealing with indigent parents and children are of little or no consequence. Many parents and children are extremely sensitive about accepting charity in any form. They are unwilling to subject themselves to possible pity or scorn by accepting free textbooks unless they are supplied free to all children.

4

Textbooks remain one of the chief causes of public criticism of the schools. Of all school expenses the only one that falls directly on the individual is the expense of textbooks. All other expenses are borne out of general school taxes. Uniformity of textbooks and long-term adoptions came about originally because the cost of textbooks was a direct personal expense. When textbooks are furnished free the demand for uniformity is less and desirable changes may be made more frequently without stirring up public opposition. Supplementary books and a larger variety of appropriate books of all kinds may be furnished under the free textbook plan without arousing public opposition.

5

Textbooks cost less when they are purchased by the city, the county, or the state than they do when they are purchased from dealers by individuals. This is true because they are bought in larger quantities and distributed directly to the pupils through the schools without additional expense or profit. Moreover, fewer books are needed because each book, under the free textbook plan, is used up. Under individual ownership very few books are entirely used up.

6

Free textbooks increase school attendance, especially in the upper grades where the burden of buying books is heaviest and where the tendency to drop out is greatest.

D. AGAINST FREE TEXTBOOKS

1

Under the free textbook plan, after the first year of use, books become second-hand. They become increasingly dirty and unattractive with each additional year of use until they finally fall apart. The child has no feeling of personal ownership for these books and hence he has no incentive for taking care of them. Soiled and unattractive books are repugnant to the finer sensibilities of children, even as they are to adults. They cannot but fail to stimulate the natural interest that a clean new book arouses in the normal child.

Not only are free textbooks usually dirty and unattractive, but they may well be disease germ carriers. No satisfactory plan has been devised thus far for successfully fumigating or disinfecting textbooks.

Rebuttal. Free textbooks furnished as public property can be kept more sanitary and attractive than can privately owned books. Under private ownership the teacher can have very little to say about the abuse of books, whereas under public ownership she can demand reasonable care of them. They afford an excellent opportunity to inculcate the habit of respect for public property. Under proper management textbooks furnished at public expense will last longer and remain more sanitary and attractive than will privately owned books.

2

Free textbooks greatly increase the burden of taxation for school purposes, and thereby awaken public opposition to the schools. Money which might better be spent for teachers' salaries and for necessary educational supplies is diverted to textbooks which could and should be bought by the individual.

Rebuttal. In no case is the cost of textbooks more than two or three per cent of the total amount spent for teachers' salaries and the increase in taxation is practically negligible. In the long run a community actually pays less for its textbooks when they are furnished free than it does under the individual ownership plan.

3

Under the free textbook plan, children are deprived of the use of textbooks during the vacation period. It is assumed that it is desirable for children to continue their studies, to some extent at least, during the vacation period.

4

When textbooks are furnished free they are merely loaned to pupils. The child has no feeling of personal ownership such as he would have if the books belonged to him. He is not encouraged to build up a library of his own and thereby to acquire what may become a permanent wholesome interest.

5

The free textbook plan of operation makes it necessary for schools to set up more or less elaborate machinery to distribute and account for textbooks. This imposes an additional burden on teachers who are already heavily burdened, and thereby decreases their teaching efficiency.

6

Free textbooks encourage the public to depend upon the state. Self-reliance and resourcefulness are discouraged in the degree that the state does for an individual what he can readily do for himself. In the case of indigents, free textbooks might be supplied, but there is no reason for indiscriminate almsgiving which is everywhere recognized as doing more harm than good. There is really no more reason for the state or the community to furnish free textbooks than there is for the state or the community to furnish free food or clothing. Food and clothing are just as essential to school attendance as are textbooks.

Rebuttal. Precisely the same arguments might be made against free schools or free bridges or free fire departments. None of them is really free. They are all tax supported. Textbooks are a part of the necessary educational machinery, whereas food and clothing are not. The latter would be necessary even if there were no schools.

CRITERIA FOR A UNIFORMITY LAW

It seems probable that each of the foregoing arguments has some basis in fact. Under certain conditions each of them might very well be valid. Their validity can be determined only in the light of given local conditions. It is evident that some of the arguments presented here have more weight than others, and that a single advantage claimed on one side may offset several disadvantages claimed on the other side.

For the purposes of this study it is not necessary to evaluate these advantages and disadvantages, or to weigh them against each other. They may all be accepted as valid. They point out benefits which should be retained and objections which should be met in a model textbook law. They may be regarded as criteria for the formulation of a textbook law which will retain most of the advantages of uniformity without the disadvantages.

For the sake of clarity and brevity the arguments both for and against uniformity are stated below in positive form. That is, they are offered as criteria for the evaluation of the textbook law which will be proposed for Florida.

1. The prices of books under the proposed plan must be as low as they would be under any other sound plan.
2. The selection of textbooks must be made by a competent professional body.
3. The proposed plan must provide against losses when families move from one district to another.
4. Textbooks must be selected with reference to courses of study.
5. The books selected must fit the particular needs of the schools which will use them.
6. The proposed law must provide for dropping unsatisfactory textbooks and for replacing them with satisfactory books within a reasonable time.
7. Under the proposed plan the term of adoption must be flexible.
8. Local districts must be given as much freedom in the management of their own schools as they are capable of exercising wisely and effectively.

A uniformity law which will satisfy these criteria should be acceptable to those who favor uniformity as well as those who oppose uniformity.

CRITERIA FOR A FREE TEXTBOOK LAW

The arguments for and against free textbooks do not lend themselves so readily to treatment as criteria for a model law as do the arguments for and against uniformity. This is true because the issues have not been so definitely joined. The opponents of free textbooks do not deny the advantages claimed for the plan by its supporters; instead, they set up certain disadvantages. That these disadvantages are not fatal is indicated by the definite trend in favor of free textbooks. As was shown in Table 2, twenty states now have mandatory free textbook laws and twenty-three other states have permissive free textbook laws.

The term *textbooks* as here used includes not only basal textbooks but also supplementary books and reference books, maps, charts, globes, and all other instructional supplies necessary to carry on the educational process. The arguments presented in favor of and against free textbooks apply with equal force to all other necessary instructional supplies. Textbooks are merely *some* of the tools used in the educational process. There are tools other than textbooks which may be just as essential as textbooks. If the free textbook plan is adopted, it should be interpreted to include whatever instructional supplies may be necessary to carry out the evident intent of the law.

This interpretation is already commonly made in many of the cities that furnish free textbooks. That it is not an unreasonable interpretation of the meaning of the term is shown by a state supreme court decision cited by Hamilton in his study, *The Courts and the Curriculum.*[1] The decision was as follows:

> "The general question is whether the words 'school supplies,' found in the tenth section of the act, is embraced within the meaning of the term 'textbooks.' 'School supplies,' as used in this act, means maps, globes, and other apparatus necessary for use in schools, and we think that a chart or a map or a globe is as much a textbook as a reader or speller, within the purposes and intention of the act under consideration. We do not think that the term 'textbooks' should be given a technical meaning, but that it is comprehensive enough to and does include globes, maps, charts,

[1] Hamilton, Otto Templar. *The Courts and The Curriculum*, p. 135. Bureau of Publications, Teachers College, Columbia University, 1927.

pens, ink, paper, etc., and all other apparatus and appliances which are proper to be used in the schools in instructing the youth; and we conclude, therefore, that the act under consideration is not broader than its title, and that the term 'school supplies,' found in the tenth section of the act, is not foreign to the term 'textbooks' found in the title of the act, but is germane to, and comprehended and included within the term 'textbooks.' "

Summarizing various court decisions with reference to free instructional supplies, Hamilton says: [2]

1. The trend of the decisions shows a departure from the early practice of requiring that all purchases of "general instructional equipment" be authorized by the previous vote of the electors of the district toward the practice of giving the local officials full control of such matters.

a. The decisions show a trend toward approval of the requirement that such purchases be provided for in an annual estimate to be presented by the purchasing officials to the electors or an advisory board.

2. There is a decided trend in the decisions towards being increasingly liberal in construing the statutory powers of school officials in purchasing whatever general instructional equipment the best interests of the children of the schools demand.

Since the experience of the states that have adopted the free textbook plan seems to have been generally satisfactory, and since the trend is in the direction of mandatory free textbooks to a marked extent, it seems reasonable to conclude that a model textbook law will include provision for mandatory free textbooks. Accordingly, the feature of mandatory free textbooks is set up as one of the criteria for a model textbook law.

The criterion here proposed implies free textbooks and free instructional supplies for all grades. There seems to be no valid educational reason for limiting this provision to the elementary grades, as is now the practice in Florida. Secondary schools are just as much a part of the free public school system as are elementary schools, and every child is just as much entitled to a high school education as he is entitled to an elementary school education. The fact that the compulsory school attendance law does not apply to the higher grades does not relieve the state or the local community of their obligations in this respect. The compulsory attendance law sets up a *minimum* standard—not a desirable standard.

[2] *Op. cit.*, p. 131.

If it should appear that the financial condition of Florida does not warrant at this time the extension of the free textbook plan to include textbooks and other educational supplies for all grades, provisions should be made for the gradual introduction of the plan.

CHAPTER V

STATE RESPONSIBILITY FOR TEXTBOOKS

This chapter will deal primarily with the fundamental relationship which exists between the state and the local community with respect to responsibility for education. Starting with the generally accepted proposition that education is a function of the state, and that the state must accept responsibility for a minimum program of education, it is hoped that certain corollary principles may be developed which will have direct bearing on the question of the relationship that should exist between the state and the local community in the matter of textbook selection and provision.

It goes without saying that the state, subject only to the state constitution, is the source of authority over all public schools in the state. State, county, and local boards of education are creatures of the state, legally speaking, and they are responsible to the state. Whatever authority they may have is conferred on them or delegated to them by the state.

For administrative reasons the state has retained for itself certain specific authorities over the schools of the state. Certain other authorities and responsibilities have been delegated to the state department of education, and still others to district or local boards of education. The principle upon which the state retains or delegates authority is not well defined. What may be a local function in one state is a state function in another, while in the third it may be a function of the state board of education. Although the principle is not well defined it is evidently generally operative, both in theory and in practice. Schmidt [1] shows that certain authorities are generally retained by the state; that certain others are generally delegated to the state department of education; and that certain others are generally delegated to the local board of education.

[1] Schmidt, W. E. *The Development of a State's Minimum Educational Program.* To be published by Bureau of Publications, Teachers College, Columbia University.

If the state is to be responsible for a minimum program in education it must define that program in terms of standards or requirements of some sort; otherwise the phrase *minimum program* is meaningless. The state may define its minimum program by specific legislation, or it may delegate the authority and responsibility for doing so to its constituted agents. The elements which must be considered in defining the minimum program are those which are essential to the educational process. The state could not discharge its responsibility for a minimum educational program merely by providing the necessary money. There would have to be assurance that such money was judiciously and effectively spent.

The elements which will be included in a minimum program will of necessity be different in different states. They may be different in the same state at different times. Social and economic conditions are constantly changing, and what may seem to be an educational fad to-day may be an educational necessity a few years hence.

In his study *State Support of Public Schools,*[1] Mort proposes four criteria for choosing the elements of a minimum program. The first criterion proposed is that of *universality*. That is to say, educational features which are common to all communities in the state should be included in the minimum educational program. The precise elements which should be included in such a program may vary widely, but no matter how variable these elements may be, there are some that must be included in any effective educational program.

Teachers, for example, are essential to the educational process. Provision should be made, therefore, in the minimum program to insure for every school in the state teachers whose qualifications are at least up to the minimum standard. This particular element is generally provided for in the several states under certification laws, the administration of which is usually delegated to the state department of education. This does not mean that the requirements are uniform for every teacher in the state. Standards for high school teachers may not be the same as those for elementary school teachers, or for teachers of special subjects. Moreover, different standards may be prescribed for different types or

[1] Mort, Paul R. *State Support of Public Schools*, p. 8. Bureau of Publications, Teachers College, Columbia University, 1926.

classes of schools within the state. Local districts are free to employ any teacher whose qualifications equal or exceed the minimum standard. The state's responsibility ceases when the local district accepts or goes beyond the minimum standard.

Courses of study are essential to the educational process. Provisions should be made, therefore, to insure for every school in the state courses of study which will include at least the minimum essentials in education. As in the case of certification laws the administration of this element is usually delegated to the state department of education. This does not mean a uniform course of study throughout the state. Different types of schools may have different courses of study. The more progressive schools will certainly exceed the minimum requirements. Each local district remains free to develop its own course of study, so long as the prescribed minimum essentials are included in it. State responsibility ceases when the local community accepts or exceeds the minimum course of study.

A third element which is essential to the educational process as it now operates is textbooks. Without textbooks many teachers would be seriously handicapped in administering courses of study. Should not provisions be made, therefore, to insure for every school in the state textbooks which are at least up to the minimum standard? This would not necessarily mean a uniform series of textbooks which every school in the state would be required to use. Different types or classes of schools may need different types of textbooks. Local districts might be permitted to choose the books which they consider best adapted to their own requirements, provided such books were equal to or better than the books prescribed in the minimum standard, just as they are free to select their own teachers and to develop their own courses of study, provided the state's minimum requirements are met or exceeded.

In the states that have provided for state control of textbooks the common practice is to delegate authority and responsibility to the state board of education or to a specially appointed commission. These bodies usually prescribe a single list of textbooks which all the schools in the state are required to use. The principle of state responsibility for a minimum program, with the privilege of going beyond the minimum granted to local districts is thus denied. The minimum is also the maximum. There can be no possibility of further growth so far as textbooks are concerned under such a system.

In the states that have not provided for state control of textbooks the common practice is to allow each district to choose its own books without reference to standards of any sort. In these states districts that have competent professional leaders may be capable of selecting textbooks adapted to their own requirements, quite as well without standards as they would be with standards.

If all schools were conducted under competent professional leadership, there would be no occasion for states to set up standards for minimum educational programs, except for the purpose of equalizing the tax burden. The final solution for many perplexing educational problems may lie in the development of some plan of organization which will provide competent professional leadership and supervision for all schools; but until some such plan is developed and until such leaders and supervisors are provided for all the schools, the state must make some provision to protect less fortunate districts against themselves.

Minimum standards are needed in such districts. If the state fails to set up standards, then it has failed in its responsibility to these districts for a minimum program in education.

If state prescription of a single list of textbooks is objectionable because it denies the progressive school district the right to use better books than those on the prescribed list; and if no prescription at all is objectionable because it fails to protect the less fortunate district against itself, the logic of the situation seems to demand that the state set up, through its constituted agents, minimum standards which must be met by all districts in the state but which may be exceeded by any district that chooses to do so. Such action would be in accord with what all states have already done in relation to teacher certification and state courses of study. Moreover, the principle involved here is fundamental in the government of the United States, not only in school affairs but also in state and local government.

Because of the difficulty (if not the present impossibility) of setting up objective standards for textbooks, such as have been set up for qualifications of teachers and for courses of study, it may be more feasible, until such objective standards are developed, to prescribe minimum standards for textbooks in terms of other textbooks which are acceptable. This implies a multiple list of textbooks for each subject and each grade, any one of which would meet the minimum standard. It also implies the right of any district to select for its own use books not on the approved multiple list, provided the district could show that such books were more suitable for its needs than those on the approved list.

This plan seems to be in harmony with the general proposition of state responsibility for a minimum educational program, and at the same time in harmony with the fundamental proposition that the local district should have as complete control over its own affairs as it is capable of administering effectively. It is, therefore, offered as another criterion for evaluating a model textbook law. It may be restated as follows: The model textbook law must provide a multiple list of textbooks for each subject and each grade, from which local districts or other supervisory units may make selections. Districts which have peculiar needs not met by books on the approved multiple list may on proper showing adopt other books.

One of the criteria previously set up for evaluating a model textbook law is the feature of mandatory free textbooks. What should be the state's financial responsibility in this connection, in addition to and beyond the mandate requiring that textbooks be furnished to pupils free of charge? As a part of the state's responsibility for a minimum program in education, there is the responsibility for equalizing the tax burden necessary to support the minimum program. If it is conceded that textbooks should be included among the essential elements in a minimum program, then it follows that the state should finance textbooks on the same basis and to the same extent that it finances other features included in the minimum program. There is no more and no less reason for the state to furnish free textbooks than there is for the state to furnish free teachers or free school buildings. State responsibility for financing the minimum program, whatever the elements may be that are included in that program, is discharged when it equalizes the tax burden necessary to support such a program.

CHAPTER VI

THE PROPOSED TEXTBOOK LAW FOR FLORIDA

This chapter will deal primarily with the general provisions which should be included in the proposed textbook law for Florida, in accordance with the criteria proposed and in the light of the present status of textbook legislation in Florida.

THE CRITERIA

The criteria set up in Chapters III, IV, and V for evaluating the proposed textbook law for Florida, stated in a somewhat different order, are as follows:

1. The state should set up, through its constituted agents, minimum standards for textbooks.
2. Authority to set up standards and to make regulations concerning textbook selection should be vested in a competent, responsible, and professional body.
3. Standards for textbooks should be set up in the form of approved multiple lists for each subject and each grade.
4. Local districts should be permitted to select textbooks from the approved multiple list to suit local needs. Local districts that have peculiar needs not met by books on the approved list should be permitted to adopt other textbooks, on proper showing.
5. The term of adoption should be flexible. Districts should be free to change books when the best interests of their schools will be served by doing so.
6. The cost of textbooks under the proposed plan should not be greater than it would be under any other plan.
7. All textbooks, supplementary books, reference books and other necessary instructional supplies should be furnished to all public school pupils free of charge.
8. To the extent that such textbooks, supplementary books, reference books and other instructional supplies are essential to the realization of the state's minimum educational program, the

state should assume responsibility for equalizing the tax burden necessary to furnish them.

9. Local districts should be given as much freedom in the management of their schools as they are capable of exercising wisely and effectively.

10. The proposed law should conform to the native characteristics, institutions, and economic conditions of Florida.

ITEMS TO BE PROVIDED FOR

The items which should be provided for in the proposed textbook law for Florida are those which are found in textbook laws in the uniformity states. A composite list of such items appears on pages 12 and 13 of this study, followed by a brief explanation of how it was derived.

The justification for the use of these items lies in the fact that in the states which have uniformity laws such laws are framed in terms of the items here proposed. It is reasonable to suppose that the composite list represents the experience of the several uniformity states over a comparatively long term of years with reference to the items which need to be provided for in textbook legislation.

In order to formulate the proposed textbook law for Florida, it remains, then, to consider each of the items in the composite list in the light of the criteria set up and in the light of the present status of textbook legislation in Florida.

1

The Adopting Body.—The criterion proposed for the adopting body provides that authority to set up standards for textbooks and to make regulations concerning them should be vested in a competent, professional body.

The state department of education, under the general authority of the state board of education, seems to meet the requirements of this criterion quite fully. The members of the state superintendent's staff are necessarily familiar with educational conditions throughout the state. They must be professionally trained if they are to discharge their duties efficiently. They must be nonpartisan and nonpolitical by the very nature of their offices.

To delegate authority over textbooks to the state department of education would be in accord with the generally approved practice of making this department responsible for administering the state's minimum educational program. There is no apparent reason why the state department should have less authority over textbooks than it has over teachers and courses of study. Under the proposed textbook law, the duties of the adopting or selecting body would be primarily administrative. The necessary administrative machinery is already developed in the state department. There is no good reason why the state should complicate its educational machinery by the appointment of a special textbook commission when it has at hand an agent which is likely to be as competent as any the state can appoint.

In Florida, authority over textbooks is vested in the board of commissioners of state institutions. A subcommission composed of seven educators recommends to the board of commissioners, but the latter body may disregard such recommendations if it chooses to do so. The board of commissioners of state institutions is composed of six members appointed by the governor. The state superintendent of public instruction is not a member of this board. None of the members is engaged in or professionally trained for educational work.

The designation of the state department of education to administer the textbook laws of the state would be logical and at the same time would satisfy the standards previously set up. It is proposed, therefore, that one of the general provisions of the textbook law for Florida shall be that the state department of education shall have authority to set up minimum standards for all textbooks used in the public schools of the state and to make all regulations necessary to carry out the evident intent of the law not otherwise specifically provided for.

2

Scope and Effect.—As was indicated in the previous section, the proposed law would apply to all public schools in the state and to all grades and all subjects provided for in the minimum program. As to the nature of the standards to be set up, the criterion suggests that they be described in terms of a multiple list of acceptable textbooks for each grade and each subject. The exact number of books which should be approved for a given subject or grade will vary as conditions vary within the state. In general the state department of education should attempt to select books for the approved list which will be suitable for the different types and classes of schools in the state. The state department should bear in mind the necessity for providing local districts with adequate lists to choose from.

The number of books on the approved list need not be as large for some subjects as for others. Until experience indicates otherwise, a minimum of three and a maximum of six or seven textbooks on the approved list is suggested for each subject and each grade.

In Florida a single list of textbooks is prescribed. Schools that are in session for five months in a year must use the same books that the nine-month school uses. The prescribed textbook in agriculture must be used alike in both the southern and the northern sections of the state, although their agricultural necessities and possibilities are entirely different. The large city high school with its shops, laboratories, libraries, and staff of specialist teachers uses the same textbooks that the small two- or three-teacher rural high school uses. Even if none of these considerations has weight, there is still the disadvantage that grows out of the fact that the teachers who use the books have had no part in their selection.

A multiple list of approved textbooks from which local districts might select would tend to relieve most of these difficulties.

3

Term of Adoption.—According to the criterion set up for this item, the term of adoption should be flexible. It should be possible for any district to discontinue within a short time the use of any textbook which proves unsatisfactory. Even when the adopted books are satisfactory there is no valid reason why they should all be adopted for the same term of years. One reasonable basis for determining the length of the adoption period is the life of the given book. Some books are worn out much more quickly than others.

This is a matter which should be left to the local districts. It will be to their advantage to continue the use of adopted books until they are worn out. There will be no advantage in adopting books for a longer period than the life of the books.

In Florida all books are adopted for a term of eight years. No matter how unsatisfactory a textbook may prove to be, so long as the contractor fulfills his obligations the book must be used for the full adoption period. No matter what developments may take place in the fields of science, no matter how vast national and international social and political changes may be, Florida textbooks may not reflect these developments and changes during the adoption period.

Just what advantage Florida gains from an eight-year adoption period is not clear. The cost is not less than it would be under a much shorter adoption term. Books are worn out and must be replaced without reference to the adoption period. It is true that the adopting body is relieved of the burden of making new selections to some extent, but it is at the expense of the school children of the state, who are in effect denied the use of improved textbooks which may be published during the life of the long adoption period.

4

The Cost.—The criterion for this item provides that the cost of books under the proposed plan shall not be higher than the cost under any other sound plan. As is shown in Table 3, thirty-eight states already have this provision or a similar one in their textbook laws.

It is usually stipulated that the price of the adopted book shall not be greater in the adopting state than it is in any other community, district, or state in the United States; and that in case the price is lowered elsewhere in the United States, then it shall be lowered correspondingly in the adopting state.

Precisely the same price regulations are in effect in the seven non-uniformity states which follow the "open list" plan of adoptions. The approved lists in these states include practically all the textbooks published in the United States, at prices not higher than those charged in the "single list" uniformity states.

The basic price for any given textbook is the same throughout the United States. That is to say, the price which the publisher receives is the same everywhere, whether it is in a uniformity state, in a non-uniformity state, or in an "open list" state. Apparent differences in prices in different states are due primarily to differences in state laws. In one state dealers may be allowed a gross profit of only ten per cent, while in other states the law may prescribe fifteen or twenty per cent as the dealer's profit.

There may be also small differences in price due to differences in freight charges.

After allowance is made for dealer's profit and for freight charges, the price is the same everywhere *for the same book.* In some states adopted books are modified to suit the special requirements of that state. In such cases prices are adjusted accordingly.

The number of books involved in the adoption does not affect the price of the books. Texas, for example, pays as much per book for adopted books as Delaware pays, and each pays precisely the same as New England villages pay. Nor does the term of adoption affect the price of textbooks. In Kentucky, where the term of adoption is for ten years, the price of a given book is the same as it is in North Dakota, where the term of adoption is for three years.

In effect, state efforts at regulation have forced publishers to adopt uniform prices for textbooks. They may not offer lower prices in any given state than they are willing to offer in all other states with which they have or may have contracts. Large-adoption states derive no price advantages from the size of their contracts; although publishers might be willing to make concessions in view of the volume of business. On the other hand, small-adoption states and smaller units are under no disadvantage because of their size.

So far as textbook publishers are concerned, it may be assumed that they are able to protect their own interests and that they will, in the long run, make a reasonable profit, no matter what laws are passed. They must do so if they are to remain in business. From the standpoint of the state, price-fixing laws are not wholly satisfactory. Originally, there may have been ample justification, as well as merit, in the efforts of the various states to regulate prices of textbooks, but it is evident to-day that such laws have no practical effect on prices, so far as individual states are concerned.

Most uniformity states provide in their textbook laws for the exchanging of books. Publishers are required to state in their bids the amount they will allow on books of the old series in exchange for books in the new series. This is essentially a matter of price, and as such is covered in the preceding discussion. It may be worth noting, however, that the number of books which will be turned in for exchange when new books are adopted is not likely to be very large. In Florida the value of all the elementary books turned in for exchange after the 1924 adoption in which eight books were changed was only $1,162.60, although the exchange period was two years instead of the customary one year. The sales of adopted books for the year 1925-26 amounted to $638,891. The implications are that the importance of exchange provisions is not great, and that adopting bodies should not be misled, when they are considering prices, by apparently favorable exchange prices.

5

Exemptions.—While no specific criterion was set up for this item, by implication it is covered in criterion No. 4 which provides that local districts that have needs not met by textbooks on the approved list should on proper showing be permitted to adopt other books. Criterion No. 2 authorizes the state department of education to make all necessary regulations not otherwise provided for. The state department would, therefore, have authority to decide what would constitute a proper showing. It may not be possible or even desirable for the state department to make specific regulations in advance to cover such cases. If the approved list of textbooks is reasonably adequate, it is not probable that there would be many applications for exemption. Until experience proves the contrary, it would seem best to decide each case on its own merits.

6

Administrative Procedure and Legal Safeguards.—Authority to make all rules and regulations not prescribed by law is vested in the state department of education under the criteria herein proposed. This plan is already in operation in ten states, as is shown in Table 3. In substance the adopting bodies in these states are authorized to make all rules and regulations not in conflict with other provisions which may be necessary to carry out the essential features of the law with reference to selecting, adopting, contracting for, distributing, and enforcing the use of the prescribed textbooks. It is not necessary to complicate the textbook law by providing in the law for details which can be left to the state department of education. That the items included under the general heading of administrative procedures and legal safeguards can be safely left to the state department of education is amply demonstrated by the experience of the states which follow that plan.

In Florida many of the administrative features of textbook selection are now left to the textbook commission. Such matters as advertising for bids, requiring sealed bids, the form of the bid, and regulations pertaining to the distribution of books are now in the hands of the state textbook commission. The law prescribes the amount of the bond to be required of successful bidders, provides for a state textbook depository and for county depositories, and exacts penalties for violations of the various provisions of the law.

7

Free Textbooks.—The proposed textbook law must provide for free textbooks for all pupils in all public schools in the state, in accordance with the criteria proposed for this item. The word *textbook* is defined to include not only basal textbooks but also all necessary supplementary books, and other educational supplies. The local supervisory or administrative unit should bear the expense of furnishing free textbooks and other educational supplies, although the state should equalize the tax burden necessary to support its minimum educational program, which program should include the free textbooks and other educational supplies necessary to carry out the program. In Florida the supervisory unit is the county; accordingly the expense of free textbooks and other educational supplies should be borne by the county out of the county school fund which should be equalized by the state.

If this plan were adopted, textbooks and other educational supplies would be the property of the county school district. The county school authorities would be responsible for distributing and accounting for them, and for prescribing such rules and regulations as might be necessary to insure reasonable care of them. This plan is already in operation in twelve states, as is shown in Table 3. That is, twelve states have mandatory free textbook laws under which the local district is required to furnish textbooks free of charge. Nine of these thirteen states have had such laws for more than twenty-five years. It is reasonable to suppose that the experience of these states has been satisfactory, inasmuch as their free textbook laws have remained substantially unchanged since they were enacted.

In Florida, free textbooks are furnished for only the first six grades. They are paid for by the state out of the proceeds of a special tax levied for that purpose. The state law providing for free textbooks also prescribes the method of distributing and accounting for them.

SUMMARY

The proposed textbook law for Florida will include the following general provisions:

1. The state department of education, under the state board of education, shall have authority to select textbooks for use in all the public schools of the state, and to make all rules and regulations necessary to carry out the manifest intent of the textbook law.

2. The state department of education shall approve for use in all the public schools in the state multiple lists of textbooks for each grade and each subject prescribed in the state course of study. County districts shall have the right to choose from such approved lists, subject to the approval of the state department of education. It is specifically provided that the adopted textbooks need not be uniform within any county or local district.

The approved list shall consist of not less than three and not more than seven textbooks, appropriate for each grade and for each school subject prescribed in the state course of study.

Local districts shall have the right to use books other than those on the approved list when it may appear to the state department of education that the needs of such local districts are not adequately served by books on the approved list.

3. The term of years for which any textbook shall be adopted shall be determined by the county school officials. Terms of adoption need not be uniform for all books or for all grades. County school officials shall have authority to drop unsatisfactory textbooks at the close of any school year, and, subject to the approval of the state department of education, to adopt other books from the approved list, as their interests may appear, provided the state department of education shall first be notified in writing of the proposed change, together with the specific reasons therefor.

4. The state department of education shall not consider any textbook for the approved list until the publisher of such textbooks has filed with the state department of education an affidavit showing the lowest price at which said textbook is sold anywhere in the United States under similar conditions of distribution; and no textbook shall be placed on the approved list until the publisher has executed a suitable contract and filed a suitable bond, as the state department of education may require, to furnish said textbook at the price and for the term of years agreed on by the state department of education and the publisher.

5. The county school district shall furnish textbooks and all other necessary educational supplies without charge to all pupils attending the public schools within the county subject to such rules and regulations as the county school officials may prescribe.

6. Free textbooks and other necessary educational supplies shall be included in and considered a part of the state's minimum educational program.

BIBLIOGRAPHY

Chapter I

School codes of the several states for the years 1905-07, 1915-17, 1925-27.

U. S. Commissioner of Education, *Annual Report,* 1896-97, Vol. 2, pp. 1538-40; 1897-98, Vol. 1, pp. 893-908; 1899-1900, Vol. 2, pp. 2603-12; 1902, Vol. 2, pp. 2390-94; 1903, Vol. 2, pp. 2415-17; 1905, p. 194.

U. S. Bureau of Education, Bulletin, 1915, No. 36; 1923, No. 50.

Cubberley, E. P. *State School Administration,* Chap. XXI. Houghton Mifflin, 1927.

Chapter II

Current school codes of the several states.

U. S. Bureau of Education, Bulletin, 1915, No. 36.

Cubberley, E. P. *State School Administration,* Chap. XXI, Houghton Mifflin, 1927.

Chapter III

Florida School Laws, 1885 to 1927.

Florida School Reports, 1869 to 1926.

Chapter IV

1. Allan, D. A. "Free Textbooks. An Opposing View." *American School Board Journal,* 59:87, 89-90, Nov., 1919.
2. Andrews, E. B. "Free School Books." *Cosmopolitan,* 32: 329-33, Dec., 1902.
3. Avery, L. B. "State Printed Textbooks in California." *Elementary School Journal,* 19: 628-33, April, 1919.
4. Baker, G. M. "Texts on Textbooks." *School Board Journal,* 48: 58-59, Aug., 1919.
5. Board of Superintendents, New York City. "Free Textbooks in the New York City High Schools." *School and Society,* 2: 557-58, Oct. 16, 1915.
6. Brown, John F. "State Publication of School Books." *School and Society,* 2: 474-85, Oct. 2, 1915.
7. Brown, John F. "Textbooks and Publishers." *Elementary School Journal,* 19: 382-88, Jan., 1919.
8. Brown, John F. *State Publication of School Books.* Macmillan, 1915.
9. Brown, G. E. "Should the State Publish Its Own Textbooks?" *Journal of Education,* 81: 566-67, May 27, 1915.
10. Butcher, T. W. "Some Difficulties Attending the Work of a Textbook Commission." *Elementary School Journal,* 19: 500-05, March, 1919.
11. Carr, John W. *State Uniformity Laws,* pp. 280-84. National Education Association, Washington, D. C., 1908.

12. CAST, G. C. "Selecting Textbooks." *Elementary School Journal,* 19: 468-72, Feb., 1919.

13. CHANCELLOR, WM. E. "The Government Publication of School Books." *School Journal,* 81: 161-64, March, 1914.

14. CHANCELLOR, WM. E. "The State Publication Question." *School Journal,* 80: 218-20, April, 1913.

15. CLAXTON, P. S. *Further Reasons for Federal Aid to Elementary Education.* Child Labor Bulletin, 6: 66-71, May, 1917.

16. COX, E. M. "Free Textbooks." *Western Journal of Education,* 88-98, Feb., 1903.

17. CRISSEY, FOREST. "Expensive Free Education." *Saturday Evening Post,* December 14, 1912.

18. CUBBERLEY, E. P. "A Distinctive American Achievement in Education." *Educational Progress Bulletin,* Vol. 5, No. 2, Jan., 1926.

19. CUBBERLEY, E. P. *State School Administration.* Chap. XXI, pp. 555-81. Houghton Mifflin, 1927.

20. DANNER, V. E. "The Case for Free Textbooks." *Oklahoma Journal of Education,* 6: 6-10, Dec. 9, 1916.

21. DEWEY, HENRY B. "Adoption and Purchase of Textbooks." *American School Board Journal,* 60: 39-40, March, 1920.

22. DEWEY, HENRY B. "Textbook Legislation—Its Inconsistencies and Injustice—the Remedy." *American School Board Journal,* 60-61: 31-32, January, 1920.

23. DOUGHTON, ISAAC. "Choosing Textbooks." *American School Board Journal,* 55: 29-30, Nov., 1917.

24. EVANS, LAWTON B. "State Publication of Textbooks." *School and Home,* 6: 7-10, June, 1914.

25. FAULKNER, R. D. "The California State Textbook System." *Educational Review,* 20: 44-60, June, 1900.

26. GEDDES, J. J. "Author vs. Publisher." *Modern Language Association Publication,* 38: 95-106, 1923.

27. GINN, E. "School Books, the Publisher and the Public." *Independent,* 69: 222-25, Aug. 4, 1910.

28. HILTON, HENRY H. "Cost of Textbooks per Pupil." *Journal of Education,* 77: 369, April 3, 1913.

29. HOOD, W. R. *Textbooks.* U. S. Bureau of Education, Bulletin, 1922, 43: 19, Washington, D. C.

30. HOOD, W. R. *Free Textbooks for Public School Pupils.* U. S. Bureau of Education, Bulletin, 1923, 50: 14. Washington, D. C.

31. HUNTING, N. J. "Free Textbooks." In Nevada State Teachers' Institute and Educational Association, *Proceedings and Addresses,* 1909, 26-33.

32. Korey, A. J. "Textbooks in the Public Schools." Master's dissertation at Teachers College, Columbia University, 1909.

33. LOBIN, HENRY. "Is State Uniformity of Textbooks Desirable?" *Journal of Education,* 68: 359-60, Oct. 1, 1908.

34. MCCRAY, D. O. "Kansas, Wise and Otherwise." *Journal of Education,* 80: 200-2, Sept. 10, 1914.

35. McCray, D. O. "Textbooks Bought in Open Market." *Journal of Education.* 79: 5-6, Jan. 1, 1914.
36. McGregor, Ford H. "Free Textbooks." *American School Board Journal,* 36: 27, April, 1908.
37. McNeal, T. A. "State Publication of School Books." *School and Society,* 2: 669-70, Nov. 6, 1915.
38. Marshall, W. I. "Should the Public Schools Furnish Textbooks Free to All Pupils?" Illinois State Teachers Association, Bulletin No. 3, 1898.
39. Monahan, A. C. *Free Textbooks and State Uniformity: Bibliography,* U. S. Bureau of Education, Bulletin, 1915, 36: 1-67.
40. Monroe, Paul. *Cyclopedia of Education.* "Textbooks—Cost of Textbooks, Earliest Free Textbooks, Reasons for and Against State Uniformity," pp. 576-78. Macmillan, 1913.
41. Pattengill, H. R. "Compulsory Free Textbooks." In *Report of Michigan Superintendents,* 1898, pp. 294-96.
42. Sanders, T. E. "Renting School Books." *American School Board Journal,* 48: 28, May, 1914.
43. Shawkey, M. P. "The Adoptions of Textbooks by State, County, or District. *American Education,* 21: 402-04, April, 1918.
44. Stowe, A. Monroe. "Our Textbook Problem." *Kansas School Magazine,* 1: 201-04, May, 1912.
45. Sullivan, M. H. "State Support and Control of Education." *School and Society,* 10: 83-88, 113-17.
46. Taber, C. W. "The Publisher's Point of View Concerning the Method of Selecting Textbooks." *American School Board Journal,* 61: 29-31, 99-100, Sept., 1920.
47. Townsend, E. J. "The Textbook Question." *Education,* 11: 556-65, May, 1891.
48. Vert, E. J. "Textbooks and Public Schools." *Education,* 21: 27-31, September, 1900.
49. Waterman, S. D. "The Advantages and Disadvantages of a Free Textbook System." *Western Journal of Education,* 8: 362-66, May, 1903.
50. Winship, A. E. "State Uniformity in Textbooks." *Journal of Education,* 67: 339-42, March 26, 1908; 68: 353-56, Oct. 1, 1908.
51. Wright, E. R. "Expensive Free Education." *Publishers' Weekly,* May, 1913.

STATE REPORTS

1. California. "State Textbook Plan Reviewed." *Biennial Report,* 1909-10, pp. 59-66. W. W. Shannon, Sacramento, California.
2. Iowa. *Report of the Legislative Commission on Textbooks.* Iowa State Teachers Association, 1898.
3. Kansas. Kansas School Textbook Commission Proceedings at Special Sessions, June 17 and September 2, 1903; and regular session July 20, 1904. 1905.
4. Kansas. *Sixteenth Annual Report of State Superintendent.*
5. Michigan. *Fifty-third Report of Public Schools,* p. 24, 1902.
6. Michigan. *Report of the Hearing on School Book Legislation Before*

the Joint Committee of the Senate and House of Representatives. J. T. Griffin, Chicago, Feb. 19, 1913.
7. MINNESOTA. *School Report.* 1909-10, pp. 20, 21.
8. MISSOURI. *Fifty-third Report of Public Schools.* 1902, pp. 22-27.
9. MISSOURI. *Fifty-fifth Report of Public Schools.* 1904, p. 26.
10. ST. LOUIS, MISSOURI, BOARD OF EDUCATION. "Free Books and Stationery." *Annual Report,* 1905, pp. 241-50.
11. NEBRASKA. *Eighteenth Biennial Report,* pp. 194 ff., 1904.
12. NEBRASKA. *Nineteenth Biennial Report,* p. 85, 1906.
13. NEW YORK STATE. *Report of Investigation of the Cost of Providing Free Textbooks in the Public Schools of New York.* L. B. Lyon Co., Albany, 1915.
14. RHODE ISLAND. *Extracts from Reports on Free Textbooks.* State School Commissioner. 1893, 1898, 1907.
15. SOUTH DAKOTA. *Sixth Biennial Report,* p. 8. 1901-02.
16. SOUTH DAKOTA. *Ninth Biennial Report,* p. 318. 1907-08.
17. WISCONSIN LEGISLATURE. *Report of the Special Textbook Committee.* 1913.

UNITED STATES COMMISSIONER OF EDUCATION REPORTS

1. "The Valid Objection to Free Textbooks." *Report,* 1899-90, p. 1184.
2. "Free Textbooks—Benefits, Objections—Costs." *Report,* 1902, Vol. 1, pp. 632-40.
3. *Report,* 1911, Vol. 1, pp. 107-08.
4. *Report,* 1912, Vol. 1, p. 49.
5. *Report,* 1913, Vol. 1, pp. 916-17.
6. "Free Textbooks." *Report,* Vol. 1, p. 122.
7. "Textbooks." *Report,* Vol. 1, 1915, p. 24.
8. "Textbooks." *Report,* 1916, Vol. 1, p. 26.

UNITED STATES BUREAU OF EDUCATION BULLETINS

1. *Textbooks.* Bulletin, 1915, 23: 51-52.
2. *Textbook and Supplies—Free Textbooks—Uniformity.* Bulletin, 1915, 47: 602-26.
3. *Supply Textbooks.* Bulletin, 1915, 44: 41.
4. *Textbooks.* Bulletin, 1917, 44: 48-49, 163.
5. *Textbooks.* Bulletin, 1917, 5: 68-69.
6. Bulletin, 1919, 4: 59-68.
7. *Free Textbooks—Uniformity.* Bulletin, 1920, 30: 138-41.
8. *Textbooks and Supplies.* Bulletin, 1922, 20: 166-67.
9. *School Textbooks.* Bulletin, 1924, 36: 49-51.
10. *Free Textbooks.* Bulletin, 1925, 2: 48.

EDITORIALS

1. "The Facts About School Book Costs." *American School Board Journal,* 46: 13-14, 52, March, 1913.
2. "The State Publication of School Books." *American School Board Journal,* 71: 67, 1925.

3. "The State Printing of Textbooks." *American School Board Journal,* 74: 128, June, 1927.
4. "Kansas Decision on Textbooks." *Elementary School Teacher,* 13: 414-415, May, 1913.
5. "Criticism of Kansas Textbook Publication." *Elementary School Journal,* 17: 537-40, April, 1917.
6. "Unexpected Testimony Against Uniformity." *Journal of Education,* 77: 33-34, Jan. 9, 1913.
7. "Quality and Cost of Textbooks." *Journal of Education,* 81: 681-83, June 24, 1915.
8. "State-wide Uniformity in High School Textbooks." *Journal of Education,* 82: 119-20, August 19, 1915.
9. "State Distribution of Textbooks." *Nation,* 98: 73, Jan. 22, 1914.
10. "Textbooks and the State." *Nation,* 101: 321-22, Sept. 9, 1915.
11. "School Textbooks." *Outlook,* 110: 780-81, Aug. 4, 1915.
12. "Three Types of Textbook Troubles." *School Review,* 30: 85-87, Feb., 1922.
13. "Free Textbooks." Quoted from the *Outlook.* *School and Society,* 3: 608-10, April 22, 1916.
14. "Economizing in Textbooks." Quoted from the *Springfield Republican.* *School and Society,* 8: 294, Sept. 7, 1918.
15. "Textbook Industry." Quoted from the *New York Evening Post.* *School and Society,* 8: 380-82, Sept. 28, 1918.

MISCELLANEOUS

1. COMMITTEE ON COURSES OF STUDY AND TEXTBOOKS, NEW YORK CITY. Free Textbooks for High School Students. *School and Society,* 2: 275-76, August 21, 1915.
2. RUSSELL SAGE FOUNDATION, DIVISION OF EDUCATION. "Textbook Legislation. In its comparative study of public school systems in the forty-eight states." Publication No. 124, 1912.

CHAPTER V

1. ALEXANDER, C. "Comparative State School Aids." *Elementary School Journal,* 21: 522-28, March, 1921.
2. ALEXANDER, C. "Problem of Financing Public Education." *School and Society,* 16: 337-43, 372-8, Sept. 23-30, 1922.
3. BUTTERFIELD, E. W. "State Administration of Schools." *Journal of the National Education Association,* 362-63, 1921.
4. COOK, A. S. "What Should the People of a State Be Told About Their Schools?" *Educational Administration and Supervision,* 9: 65-74, Feb., 1923.
5. FINEGAN, THOMAS E. *Function of the State in Local Administration.* National Education Association, 348-51, 1916.
6. HARRIS, T. H. "State's Financial Responsibility to the Public Schools." *Journal of Rural Education,* 4: 348-53, April, 1925.
7. MORT, PAUL R. "Needed Research in the Field of State Aid." *Teachers College Record,* 27: 707-12, April, 1926.

8. MORT, PAUL R. *The Measurement of Educational Need.* Bureau of Publications, Teachers College, Columbia University, 1924.

9. MORT, PAUL R. *State Support for Public Schools.* Bureau of Publications, Teachers College, Columbia University, 1926.

10. STRAYER, G. D. and HAIG, R. M. "The Financing of Education in the State of New York." *Educational Finance Inquiry,* Vol. 1. Macmillan, 1923.